TOWARD A NEW MORALITY

Toward A New Morality

GERSHON G. ROSENSTOCK

PHILOSOPHICAL LIBRARY
New York

To My Children,

BRUCE, DAVID, and
SHARON

ACKNOWLEDGMENTS

I am pleased to express my profound gratitude to Mrs. Dorothy Kraitsik for her tireless efforts throughout the writing of this book. I am fortunate to have received such inspiration and service. I am also deeply grateful to Mrs. Edith Lovinger for her sustained support in the preparation of the manuscript from its initial stage until its completion. I take pride in thanking my son Bruce for his faith in the work and for his help wherever requested.

My deepest appreciation to my wife Cynthia, without whose patience and devotion this book would not have been written.

Thanks are also due to the following publishers for permission to reprint briefly from their works: Bollingen Foundation, *Two Essays on Analytical Psychology* from *The Collected Works of C. G. Jung*, translated from the German by R. F. C. Hull, Bollingen Series XX.7, Pantheon Books; Houghton Mifflin Company, *Patterns of Culture* by Ruth Benedict; and Oxford University Press, *Freedom and Reason* by R. M. Hare.

CONTENTS

INTRODUCTION

THE TRAGEDY of Hiroshima and Nagasaki has roused the man of science today from his absorption in the theoretical aspects of scientific research. The holocaust of destruction wrought indirectly by his own creative endeavors has shaken the scientist in his aloofness from his society's implementation of the creative results of his quest for truth. He has become a man of "conscience," not only deeply disturbed over the enormity of the destructive possibilities of scientific discoveries, but ready to assume direct responsibility for the applicability of scientific findings to human welfare. The man in philosophy today can do no less. In this age, when the very survival of mankind is in the balance, he must step out from the safe retreat of the contemplative life, from his preoccupation with ponderous analyses of often no more than trivia, and address himself in an intelligible manner to the urgent needs and pressing concerns of his generation.

My book is an effort in this direction. I seek to grapple with the moral implications of today's dominant society, with its mass democratization, its corporate bigness, its submergence of the individual within the organization, its creeping impersonalization, etc. My major concern is with the frightful retreat of human freedom in all areas of life and the increasing momentum of collectivism which threatens to swallow up whatever tendencies to autonomy and self-reliance may still be manifest in men and women today.

The new mass democratization has radically changed the character of our cultural institutions and rendered obsolete Dewey's institutional idealism, in which man's hope for freedom is made dependent upon the moral imperative of "idealizing" existent social institutions into tomorrow's bastions of freedom. Current trends make it unmistakably clear that any reliance for the protection of human freedom upon our present corporate social structures is a self-deceptive illusion. Thus, a realistic re-examination of the prospects of human freedom in this technological age has become an imperative demand for ethical inquiry. To do this, ethics must emerge from its current insulation within the narrowest of boundaries, namely, the logical analysis of the language of morals. It must bring to bear the latest findings in psychology, sociology, and anthropology upon the radically changed role of the individual in today's dominant society.

This is one of the objectives of my book. It centers analysis, not in abstract concepts, but in *man,* his total personality structure. I seek to establish the primacy of the ethical agent. This gives ethical inquiry a new set of questions. Instead of the traditional queries: What is the nature of the good? What is the logical meaning of basic moral terms? I propose a new set of questions: What is the nature of the ethical man? How does an individual *become* an ethical agent? In the light of these questions, we get, not only new perspectives on perennial issues in ethics, but possible answers to pressing moral problems today. These bear directly upon the role of the parent in the home, the executive in management, and the teacher in the school.

Existentialism has given priority to the concept of commitment. In a separate chapter I have attempted a contextual analysis of the moral nature of commitment as it is seen to flow from the personality structure of the individual. This gives us concrete maxims by which the ethical agent can be guided in the resolution of moral conflicts arising both from his relations to himself and to his fellow men.

My concept of the ethical man is the construction of an independent contextual analysis, in which freedom is seen, not as a ready-made human possession, but rather as the constructive attainment of a deliberate, conscious, gradually-evolving process of self-realization. In this analysis the concepts, "freedom from" and "freedom for," are filled with concrete significance and made relevant to the actualities of today. Basically I am committed to the rationality of ethics, and I seek to establish it not on abstract universal principles, but on the limited foundations of moral character. My position is one of objective relativism, in which I seek to do justice to the valid insights of both current subjectivism and objectivism.

In the first chapter, I address myself to the obdurate ethical dilemma: How can ethics achieve universality, on the one hand, and, on the other, lay down norms and goals of ethical conduct relevant and applicable to the evolving practical issues and concerns of life? I propose a contextual analysis, in which the elucidation of moral concepts is centered in the primacy of the ethical agent. I urge the fusion of ethical inquiry with the special sciences of man, and, in the light of it, conceive of freedom as a complex emergent power in man, in the process of which four distinctive dynamic aspects of character are made operative. The analysis of these four aspects of personality structure becomes the major concern of Chapters 2 to 6 inclusive.

In Chapter 2, I discuss the anthropological conception of man as the "creature" of his culture and its major antecedents in philosophical thought. Reflecting on current trends of conformity, group belongingness, and the dominance of irrationality, I seek possible solutions for the establishment of personal freedom on the limited base of the individual's own life. I propose an attitude of non-involvement, and suggest that in this dominant society, the individual give himself completely to the life task of self-fulfillment.

In Chapter 3, I seek corroboration in recent psychological findings for the thesis that we are not by native endowment committed to belongingness within a group. I set forth my position of objective relativism or ethical relativism, as distinguished from sociological relativism.

In Chapter 4, I am concerned with an analysis of the tendencies and character traits which go into the making of a dynamic personality structure, along the lines of differentiation and integration.

In Chapter 5, I seek to analyze moral reasoning's functional dependence on and organic interrelation with moral character. I elaborate on the application of the criteria of moral reasoning as implied in the primacy of the ethical agent, namely, resistance and constructivity. I seek to draw distinctions between proper moral reasoning and its pseudo-counterpart, rationalization.

In Chapter 6, I analyze the nature of moral commitment, as grounded in dynamic character. In the light of it, I attempt a critical evaluation of today's dominant ethical movement—the logical analysis of moral language.

The final chapter seeks to establish the stature of the ethical man as an emergent form of self-realization, viewing it both as an idealization of man in every age and a challenge to man, especially in our technological society. The outcome is a comprehensive view of the ethical man in his relation to himself, to others, and to God.

If my work will provoke inquiry and debate, I shall be content that its efforts have not altogether been in vain.

CHAPTER ONE

The Ethical Dilemma

THE DOMAIN of ethics has been beset by an obdurate dilemma which is not likely to be resolved so long as ethical inquiry remains un-mindful of what we shall call the Fallacy of Misplaced Primacy. The dilemma involves this basic problem: How can ethics achieve universality on the one hand, and, on the other, lay down norms and goals of ethical conduct relevant and applicable to the evolving practical issues and concerns of life? Persistent efforts to resolve the dilemma have, by and large, proven more confusing than enlighten-ing. Traditionally, ethical writers have centered their analyses on the concepts of good, bad, right, and wrong, and on determining to what kind of things these predicates can be attached. Recently, in-quiry has shifted to an analysis of the language of ethics. Both these types of analysis are strictly formal and fail to recognize what is primary in every ethical situation—namely, the ethical man. This failure we call the Fallacy of Misplaced Primacy.

The construction of barren generalizations inapplicable to the concrete ethical experience; the hypostatization of a culture's supreme values into ultimate universal goods; the reliance on intuition for the ground of ethical certainty; the reduction of the "ought" to non-ethical determinations; the insistence on the relativity of ethical values; the denial of the cognitive import of ethical statements—these typify the dubious escape-routes from the ethical dilemma of achiev-ing, at once, generality and practicality. Rather than avenues to clarity, they are blind-alleys leading to greater perplexity.

If a breakthrough in ethics is to come (and the sense of crisis and the increasing demand for "radically new beginnings" in philos-ophy make it imminent), it may well hinge on the recognition of the Fallacy of Misplaced Primacy.

The crucial need for the shift of primacy to the ethical agent comes to the fore once we take note of the place of freedom in ethical experience. Without freedom, no ethics is possible. There can be no ethical act which is not freely willed. There can be no ethical sentiment which is not freely felt. There can be no ethical judgment which is not freely formed. There can be no ethical norms or goals which are not freely chosen. Freedom, then, is the indispensable foundation for the construction of ethical concepts and theories. Obviously, freedom's locus-operandus—the realm in which it comes into being and is made creatively operative—is the personality-structure of the ethical agent. Yet, in the formal approach to ethical values, the ethical agent is more often than not merely tacitly presupposed. It seems evident, on logical grounds alone, that what is a primary aspect in the ethical situation cannot simply be presupposed, but warrants, instead, careful analysis and explication.

In current ethical debate the issue, even, of whether or not man is free has been a controversy in abstract formalistic terms. It involves such topics as: determinism vs. indeterminism; freedom of will vs. compulsion; the distinction between natural laws as *descriptions* of natural processes and moral laws as *prescriptions* of human conduct. To the layman, the difference between freedom and compulsion is a fact which he finds exemplified every day. To his mind, there is no actual problem here; some of his actions are free while others are compelled or constrained. His experience has demonstrated to him that he is free when he abstains from an intended action, or when his actions are under his control. On the other hand, he has been in situations where he has felt a compulsion to do something which he had no intention of doing.

The layman, however, may lack a knowledge of the criteria by which to determine what type of free action is regarded as an ethical one. What most people seem unaware of is the fact that ethical freedom, so far from being a ready possession, is an achievement which one must realize by one's own bold efforts in a persistent struggle against seemingly unconquerable obstacles. Unless a man establishes this freedom in his own life, he cannot hope to qualify as an ethical agent. It becomes, therefore, a primary objective for ethical inquiry to provide the layman with concrete directives to guide him in the battle for ethical freedom.

Thus, the shift of primacy to the ethical agent brings to the fore a new set of questions: What is the nature of the ethical agent? How does an individual make of himself an ethical agent? It is not altogether unwarranted to suggest that if a fresh start in ethics is to be made, it might well begin here. It is one objective of this book to demonstrate that by making the ethical agent the starting-point of inquiry, a new light is shed on the perennial issues in ethics.

A basic implication of the primacy of the ethical agent is the demand that ethical theory and social theory work together, that they reinforce each other in the analysis of the problem of how the individual can achieve ethical freedom. This means nothing less than that ethical inquiry derive its subject matter from the findings and conclusions of the social sciences in the same way as philosophy, in general, is to be grounded in scientifically established facts. For if it is true that "there is no philosophy where there are no special sciences," and that "in its give-and-take with the sciences, philosophy finds its function and its significance,"* then, it follows that there can be no ethics without the special sciences of man. The domain of ethics is as wide as life itself. "Morals is not a theme by itself because it is not an episode nor department by itself. It marks the issues of all the converging forces of life."** There can be no divorce between social phenomena and moral values. Is it not basically the task of ethics to make thinking men reflect critically on the morals of their culture, rather than to limit the sphere to an academic elite for whom ethical discipline is often no more than the instrument of intellectual virtuosity? Perhaps traditional ethics has failed to touch the lives of men precisely because it has limited its debate to the narrow confines of abstract concepts and categories, e.g., the moral sense, will and motive, categorical imperative, and Absolute Goods. The effect of this insulation of ethics has been to remove ethical concepts from human affairs and to root them in an intellectual realm of norms and ends totally unrelated to human strivings.

Perhaps the most striking example of the divorce of ethics from the social sciences, of moral values from practical social issues, is Kant's metaphysics of morals. Caught in the dilemma be-

*See the author's book, F. A. Trendelenburg, Forerunner to John Dewey, Southern Illinois University Press, Carbondale, 1964, p. 37.

** Dewey, in Living Philosophies, World Publishing Co., 1931, pp. 31-32.

tween the universality of ethics, on the one hand, and its applicability to the concrete issues of life, on the other, Kant chose to make his primary concern universality, that is, so to construct a system of ethics that its norms, values, and laws be absolutely valid for all men everywhere. Clearly, Kant took his cue from the physical sciences of his time, whose laws were taken to be the disclosure of absolute truth. In fact, Kant was so impressed by the advance of scientific discovery that he accepted the findings of science as the presupposition and building stones of his own philosophical structure. One may say that Kant transposed the axioms of Euclidean geometry and the Newtonian laws of motion into the *a priori* structure of the human mind and the absolute foundation of scientific knowledge. So he made what he took to be the criteria of scientific lawfulness—universality and necessity—the very conditions of ethical validity.

While Kant attempted to construct, after the model of science, an absolutely valid universal system of moral laws, he was keenly aware that this would involve him in a seemingly inescapable dilemma: How can one reconcile a reign of universal law with human freedom? How can the individual be, at one and the same time, an autonomous, self-determining, ethical agent, and a subservient liege to lawful authority? For Kant the difficulty was compounded by his insistence that the scientific principle of physical causality—the necessary chain of cause-effect relations of natural phenomena—be applied to human experience as well as to the physical realm. Human nature, in its subjective passions and interests, is no less fettered by the chain of cause and effect determinations than any other aspect of nature.

In a sense, Kant's ingenious metaphysical scheme is his answer to the basic problem: How can man be, at once, morally free and psychologically determined? Kant asserted that this is possible because man is an inhabitant of two worlds—the phenomenological realm of human experience and the transcendental realm of "things-in-themselves." As a member of the transcendental realm, man can, if he so wills it, overcome the causal determinations from within and without, and make of himself an ethical being guided solely by the autonomous dictate of his own reason. While Kant set definite limits to the mind's quest for knowledge, he did not entirely cut us off from a reality beyond sense experience. As a moral thinker, he had to establish foundations in which the moral life could be securely grounded. He was keenly aware that to confine man to the empirical world is to rob him of his human dignity and his human worth. On the other hand, as an epistemologist, as one concerned with the nature and boundaries of human knowledge, he was determined to cleanse the philosophical enterprise of the excesses of pure speculation. Caught in what is, in the deepest sense, a philosopher's moral dilemma, Kant elected to retain a transcendental realm of noumena—the Greek equivalent for intelligible objects—but to specify the conditions which would make this possible. He declared that while the human mind has no access to a reality beyond, it is driven by an irresistible urge to go beyond its own limitations, to unify what we *can know* into higher all-embracing unities—the Soul, the Universe, and God. This is done by what Kant calls the power of Reason (Vernunft) in contradistinction to Understanding (Verstand), the more subordinate rational faculty which gives us our scientific knowledge.

For Kant, the products of Reason—the pure ideas of the noumenal realm—so far from reflecting a knowable reality become the ideals and regulative principles for the moral life. Man can achieve ethical freedom if he can establish a moral law which, though binding on him, does not limit his authority, but rather makes him a legislative participant in it. This he can do if he relies on Reason to provide him with universal norms that will apply to all men everywhere. He must make sure that whatever he does can in principle become a universal norm of human conduct. So Kant set down as a basic moral rule his categorical imperative: *"Act only on that maxim which will enable you at the same time to will that it be a universal law."** Here is autonomy and self-legislation tied up with the reign of universal law. The individual does the morally right because he wills it, but what he wills autonomously aims at the good of all. This is what Kant regards to be the essence of "good will." It is doing the good for the sake of goodness alone without any regard for the effects or consequences of the action. An action has genuine moral value only when it is done "out of duty" and not because some

* Immanuel Kant, *The Fundamental Principles of the Metaphysic of Ethics*, translated by Otto Manthey-Zorn, D. Appleton-Century Company, New York-London, 1938, p. 38.

inclination urges it upon us. In defining duty, Kant applies the criterion of necessity to the moral act: "Duty is the necessity of an action out of respect for the law."*

For Kant then, morality consists in willing and doing the universal, the necessary, or, in other words, the rational. Good action is rational action. If we can make our conduct consistent with a moral principle which can be made into a universal law, then we can be sure that our actions are morally good. Here is the crucial weakness of Kant's ethical system. He gives us an abstract formula and expects us to apply it to the specific moral problems which we may encounter in experience. How is this possible? Logical consistency alone does not permit us to infer something *new*, something empirical which is not already contained in the general maxim. No logical inference from general principles can tell us *what* acts or *what* ends are reasonable or universal. While Kant's universal values infuse the moral life with special dignity and nobility, they are so lofty in their moral reach as to become impracticable for guidance in actual moral situations. Clearly, by seeking to establish universality in ethics, Kant failed to do justice to ethics' role as a practical guide to human conduct. This is basically attributable to Kant's insistence that "all moral philosophy rests wholly upon its pure part."** The predominance of empty abstract generalizations and inflexible moral norms—the good will, the concept of duty, the categorical imperative—is, in the final analysis, the result of Kant's endeavor "to prepare a pure moral philosophy which has been thoroughly cleared of all that is empirical only and belongs to anthropology."*** Kant's divorce of moral values from social phenomena may give his ethical system a unique purity, but it is precisely this separation which prevents Ethics from becoming a moral force in society. If Moral Philosophy is to have an influence on human lives, it cannot be so emasculated.

While modern philosophy has come to be grounded in the physical sciences, and in recent decades has made the logical analysis of the foundations of science its major concern, it persists in the Kantian attitude of aloofness from the special sciences of man. So far from utilizing the findings of psychology, sociology, and anthropology, it

---

* *Ibid,* pp. 15-16.
** *Ibid,* p. 3.
*** *Ibid.*

has further insulated itself within the narrowest of boundaries, namely, the logical analysis of the language of morals. Within these boundaries, it takes a position of neutrality in morals,* merely examining meanings, rather than providing guide lines for a constructive ethical life. Today, when moral traditions are shaken in their foundations, and men and women are drifting aimlessly, hopelessly, devoid of a sense of an ultimate meaning of human existence, this self-withdrawal of ethical thinkers strikes one as an attitude of unconcern with the pressing needs of our time. It is one objective of this book to bring to bear current insights in the social sciences, not only on the perennial issues in ethics, but especially upon the crucial moral problems today.

It has become commonplace to decry the retreat of freedom, the decline of individualism, and the attendant dominance of collectivism even in the so-called free world today. We hear so much about the crisis of despair that we are tired of listening to one more prophetic voice of doom. Needed instead is a positive approach to the challenge of freedom, not so much as it affects our social institutions, but rather the individual men and women in our society, especially those for whom independence, individuality, and creative productivity are not just lost traits of another age. This crucial need for a constructive, realistic ethics of personal freedom underscores the primacy of the ethical agent. It reinforces our basic thesis that ethical inquiry, if it is to be adequate, must locate the focal point of its analysis in man, or, in other words, give primary consideration to the criteria and conditions required for becoming an ethical person. In respect to the issue of freedom, then, our primary problem is: How can an individual *become* free in an ethical sense?

While Kant's conception of freedom as autonomy and self-determination stands as the hallmark of ethics, it is not entirely free from the Fallacy of Misplaced Primacy. He defines freedom in purely theoretical terms, as "that property of such causality by which it can become operative without being dependent on foreign causes *determining* it."** Once we made the ethical agent the focal point of our inquiry, this definition appears to be too abstract; it does not

---

* See R. M. Hare, *Freedom and Reason*, Oxford University Press, London, 1963, pp. 87-89.
** *Ibid*, p. 65.

21

quite serve our purpose. When we ask how the individual makes of himself an ethical agent, what we then want to know is: What are the obstacles which the individual must overcome before he can achieve autonomy and self-determination? What are the forces which the individual must cultivate to become an autonomous or self-determining agent? And, finally, what is the attitude by which the ethical agent can sustain his freedom?

Thus, it becomes imperative so to define human freedom as to make it relevant to the individual who seeks to become an autonomous, self-reliant personality. For freedom is essentially an *attainment*: It is the outcome or end product of a gradually evolving, organic process in which distinct emotional and rational forces are made creatively and constructively operative.

In a preliminary sense, we may say that freedom as an attainment is a complex, emergent, psychological dynamism which, in its development, involves four distinctive processes: 1. Conscious, deliberate resistance to non-reflective determinations from within and/or without; 2. Individuation; 3. Dynamic, constructive reasoning; 4. Cultivation of a passional attitude of commitment.

These four processes are integrally entwined; however, for the purpose of analysis and proper explication they require separate treatment. The final outcome will be a comprehensive view of the ethical man in his relation to himself, to others, and to God.

CHAPTER TWO

Cultural Deterrents to Freedom

WHEN HUMAN BONDAGE is wrought by physical chains or oppressive political restraints, we need not fear for the cause of freedom. Before long, in some corner, a spark of resistance is ignited and the oppressive force is challenged by the counter-pressure of men and women who will not long endure a state of enforced servitude. The real threat to freedom, Spinoza told us, comes from a bondage of another kind, the human bondage to passion or unrestrained emotion. Although, like all rationalists, Spinoza viewed freedom as the life of Reason, he was emphatic in his insistence that we cannot expect reason alone to free us from our enslavement to passion. "An affect cannot be restrained nor removed unless by an opposed and stronger affect,"* Spinoza declares in the section "Of Human Bondage" in his *Ethic*. Mere understanding of our passions is not sufficient to remove their hold on us. To overcome the force of passion, one must mobilize the resistance of a passional counter-force. Spinoza could have predicted the recent debacle of a naive liberalism which entrusted the attainment of freedom to the processes of education and enlightenment.

The revolutionary discoveries of Freudian psychology have come to reinforce Spinoza's insight that to establish mastery over oneself there is far more involved than mere rational control over one's behavior patterns. Freud demonstrated that the fundamental attitudes of human beings in action and thought are largely determined at levels beneath that of consciousness and that the supposedly rational explanations of our attitudes are in truth but artificial "rationaliza-

---

* Spinoza, in *Spinoza Selections*, Ed. by John Wild, Charles Scribner and Sons, N. Y., Chicago, Boston, 1930, p. 292.

tions" of processes which we have failed to understand. Reason is given to us, Freud seems to say, not so much to direct our thought and action but to cloak the hidden forces which actually direct them.

Today, the findings of anthropology, sociology, and psychology provide us with a substantive knowledge of the hidden forces which control human conduct. Broadly speaking, these hidden forces or impediments to human freedom derive, on the one hand, from the political, economic and social pressures of an increasingly complex technological culture, and, on the other, from the conscious drives and unconscious compulsions of man's total subjective dynamism— that tangle of "irrationalities" which makes cowards of us all, which makes even the strongest among us conformists, or the "Organiza- tion Man."

Thus, it becomes evident that the initial phase in the battle for personal freedom is a *conscious, deliberate resistance* to the cultural and psychological determinations to which human behavior is fettered. Our concern, then, must be with the insidious, subtle deterrents to freedom from within and/or without which can be seen as the rewards for conformity or the punishments for non-conformity.

The massive, well-nigh irresistible impress of "the patterns of culture" on the formation of human character is a firmly established anthropological insight today. Ruth Benedict, one of the foremost anthropologists of our time, gives us a concise characterization of a culture's determining impact on the individual:

> The life history of the individual is first and foremost an accom- modation to the patterns and standards traditionally handed down in his community. From the moment of his birth, the customs into which he is born shape his experience and behavior. By the time he can talk, he is the little creature of his culture, and by the time he is grown and able to take part in its activities, its habits are his habits, its beliefs his beliefs, its impossibilities his impossibilities.*

Even the sophisticated among us, who like to believe that they are the creators of their own outlook and basic attitudes, are un-

---

* Ruth Benedict, *Patterns of Culture,* New American Library, N. Y., 1958, p. 18.

aware of the degree to which they are really subject to the subtle influences of their culture. Nor are they aware of the degree to which their outlook is determined by their temperamental disposition, which in turn is conditioned by cultural determinations. While we prize freedom of thought perhaps more than any other and take it to be intrinsic to the democratic society, it is for most of us, at best, an illusion and, at worst, an arrogation of crass chauvinism. The Philosopher, even, despite his unique bent of mind and professional discipline of critical thinking, reflects in his cosmic views some of the pervasive thought patterns of his culture. As William James has pointed out, a philosopher's view of man and nature is more a reflection of his temperament than an objective construction of reality.

Today, thinkers loosely grouped as the ordinary language philosophers seek to explicate the unconscious pressures reflected in the "unusual," "peculiar" or "strange" language of metaphysics. These thinkers have come to believe that it is their job "to deal with metaphysical beliefs much as a psychoanalyst deals with neuroses."[*]

In the light of all this, it is not altogether unwarranted to suppose that Kant's conception of "duty" and inflexible ethical maxims have their unconscious base in the Germanic idealization of duty and loyalty and in the peculiar temperamental constitution of his personality. It is a well-known fact that this German philosopher's habit patterns were so rigid and inflexible that the citizens of Königsberg would set their clocks by his reliable "duty" to punctuality.

While the philosopher is not entirely free from his culture's dominant influences, his special role as the critic of established traditions gives him a keen awareness, not only of the peculiar thought patterns of his culture, but also of their impact upon the lives of the people in it.

The current anthropological view of man as the "creature of his culture" has deep roots in philosophy. Perhaps the whole enterprise of philosophy can be seen as a collective endeavor of reason to transcend the limiting confines of the world into which we are born—those imposed by our culture, as well as those inherent in our native endowment. Anthropology's insight into the dominance of culture is implicit in philosophy's distinction between appearance and

---

[*] E. Pols, *The Recognition of Reason,* Southern Illinois University Press, Carbondale, 1963, p. 6.

reality, between opinion and knowledge, between a subjective view of things and an objective one. It reflects the philosopher's keen awareness that the majority of men and women in every clime and epoch are profoundly limited in an evaluation of things as they really are, and that to seize upon "truth" we must break away from established beliefs and opinions.

In his "Allegory of the Cave," Plato has given us a dramatic setting of man's complete submergence in his environment. Here we see man chained to illusions fashioned by the opinion-makers in his culture. This world of shadows is to him reality, and not even the philosopher who seeks to bring him the truth from a higher realm can break the fetters of his indoctrination.

Bacon's "Idols" gives us the same insight. Adopting Plato's symbolism, he cautioned against the "Idols of the Cave"; against the prejudices of men and women flowing from temperamental peculiarities, from education, and from their total environment. In his "Idols of the Theatre" he lashed out against worship and blind acceptance of tradition and authority.

Anthropology's view of man as the product of his culture, while anticipated throughout the classical tradition, must be attributed to the Hegelian conception of the role of man in society. In Hegel's system of thought we find an elaborate explication of the complex involvement of man in his society. Not only is man molded by his society, Hegel declared, but he is also dependent, for the fulfillment of his destiny, on the social institution of which he is an integral part. Hegel made the view of man as the creature of his society the basis of his entire philosophy. Dewey has defined this Hegelian doctrine as "institutional idealism."

For Hegel, the history of civilization is a timeless or eternal unfolding of the Absolute Spirit or Reason culminating in the attainment of freedom through the State.

> The destiny of the spiritual World, and . . . the final cause of the World at large, we allege to be the consciousness of its own freedom on the part of the Spirit, and ipso facto, the reality of that freedom. . . . This result it is, at which the process of the World's History has been continually aiming; and to which the sacrifices that have ever and anon been laid on the vast

26

altar of the earth, through the long lapse of ages, have been offered. This is the only aim that sees itself realized and fulfilled; the only pole of repose amid the ceaseless change of events and conditions, and the sole efficient principle that pervades them.*

Hegel viewed social organization as the indispensable condition of the "self-consciousness," self-expression and self-determination of the Spirit. The absolute Spirit actualizes itself in the institutions of family, law, society, and the State. Institutions are not to be seen as purely human devices for securing man's peculiar needs and ends. They are the very embodiment of Reason; they are the means by which rationality is established in action, by which the Spirit achieves its freedom. By his active participation in the institutions of his society, the individual's subjective interests and passions take on a rational, moral character. Individuals are born into a social and moral order which is not in conflict with their individuality. Man is naturally social—naturally a family man, naturally a citizen. The restrictions which the moral order in society imposes on the individual are not interferences with his nature but rather the objective fulfillment of it. So, too, the duties and obligations which are imposed upon the individual as a member of the family, society and the State are not limitations of his freedom but, on the contrary, the realization of it. In submitting to the moral law of the State, the individual does not surrender his self-determination but rather assures the establishment of it on objective grounds. His acceptance of the moral order of his society limits only the individual's subjective impulses and drives and, far from restricting human freedom, safeguards it as well as the freedom of society as a whole.

While Hegel is fully cognizant of the "Unreason" in man, he makes it the unconscious instrumentality for the self-realization of Spirit or Freedom:

The History of the World begins with its general aim—the realization of the Idea of Spirit—only in an *implicit* form (*an sich*) that is, as Nature; a hidden, most profoundly hidden,

* G. W. F. Hegel, *The Philosophy of History*, transl. by J. Sibree, Dover Publications, Inc., N. Y., 1956, pp. 19-20.

27

unconscious instinct; and the whole process of History (as already observed), is directed to rendering this unconscious impulse a conscious one. Thus appearing in the form of merely natural existence, natural will—that which has been called the subjective side—physical craving, instinct, passion, private interest, as also opinion and subjective conception—spontaneously present themselves at the very commencement. This vast congeries of volitions, interests and activities, constitute the instruments and means of the World-Spirit for attaining its object; bringing it to consciousness, and realizing it.*

One wonders whether Hegel's reliance, for the attainment of freedom, on the Absolute, on an ideal Spirit transcending the concrete individual, is actually a reflection of a deeper fear that if men were to be left to their own resources there could be no real hope for freedom. It is not altogether surprising to find Hegel, the rationalist, presenting a portrayal of the Unreason or irrationality in human society which is as frightful as that of any existentialist today:

When we look at this display of passions, and the consequences of their violence; the Unreason which is associated not only with them, but even (rather we might say *especially*) with *good* designs and righteous aims; when we see the evil, the vice, the ruin that has befallen the most flourishing kingdoms which the mind of man ever created; we can scarce avoid being filled with sorrow at this universal taint of corruption: . . . Without rhetorical exaggeration, a simply truthful combination of the miseries that have overwhelmed the noblest of nations and polities, and the finest exemplars of private virtue—forms a picture of most fearful aspect, and excites emotions of the profoundest and most hopeless sadness, counterbalanced by no consolatory result. We endure in beholding it a mental torture, allowing no defense or escape but the consideration that what has happened could not be otherwise; that it is a fatality which no intervention could alter. And at last we draw back from the intolerable disgust with which these sorrowful reflections threaten us,

---

* *Ibid*, p. 25.

28

into the more agreeable environment of our individual life—
the present formed by our private aims and interests. In short,
we retreat into the selfishness that stands on the quiet shore, and
thence enjoys in safety the distant spectacle of "wrecks con-
fusedly hurled."*

If Hegel had lived in our generation and seen his theoretical
description of history "as the slaughter-bench at which the happiness
of peoples, the wisdom of states, and the virtue of individuals have
been victimized," take on horrid reality in the unspeakably barbarous,
sadistically contrived Nazi scheme of wholesale extermination of people, he would more likely have withdrawn into the retreat "that
stands on the quiet shore" than construed all this human misery and
savagery as the necessary instrumentality for the realization of the
Spirit and the establishment of ultimate freedom.

Again, it is not altogether unwarranted to suggest that Hegel's
grand metaphysical scheme, with its Absolute Spirit actualizing itself
in nature and in history, and coming to consciousness in "great men,"
can be attributed no less to the unconscious projection of his own
ego-quest for grandeur, than to his mind's capacity to penetrate the
unfolding of history itself. It is not unlikely that Hegel saw himself
as one of the "great men" in whom the Spirit became philosophically
conscious. The fact that he selected Germany, his own culture, as
the pinnacle of civilization, the State in which politically the Spirit
achieved self-realization, reinforces this speculation. Glorifying his
own culture, he proudly wrote:

The German Spirit is the Spirit of the new World. Its aim is
the realization of absolute Truth as the unlimited self-determination of Freedom—*that* Freedom which has its own absolute form
itself as its purport. The destiny of the German peoples is to be
the bearers of the Christian principle. The principle of Spiritual
Freedom—of Reconciliation, . . . was introduced into the still
simple, unformed minds of those peoples; and the part assigned
them in the service of the World-Spirit was that of not merely
possessing the Idea of Freedom as the substratum of their reli-

* *Ibid,* pp. 20-21.

29

gious conceptions, but of producing it in free and spontaneous developments from their subjective self-consciousness.*

Sad to state, Hitler's Germany turned Hegel's glorious dream of the spiritual leadership of Germany in the world into a "concrete" incredible nightmare.

However critical one may be of Hegel's metaphysical scheme and his prophetic anticipation of freedom, his thesis of the dominance of society over the individual—the impact of social institutions on human character—must be acknowledged as an invaluable contribution to human thought. Dewey's reconstruction of Hegel's "institutional idealism" on a thoroughly naturalistic base (the "Absolute," "the self-actualization of Spirit in history," the dialectical method, etc., have disappeared) is essentially an elaboration upon the thesis that man is naturally social and that "morality is social."** Dewey is critical of those philosophies that view the "individual" and "society" as fixed discrete entities, separate and apart from each other. Much of the muddled thinking in the social sciences, he believes, has resulted from the insulation of the individual from his society, from the failure of viewing the individual as an organic part of his social environment. The very abstraction of Individual and Society has been more confusing than enlightening. When "individual" and "society" are treated as entities in themselves and factitiously separate; when the two are urged to cooperate or to remain opposed; when it is naively assumed that "in reality" their interests are mutual—then we are, in truth, posing the kind of problems which are artificial and unreal—irrelevant to the concrete problems of human existence. Abstract concepts such as "individual," "society" are for Dewey but tool-ideas or functional concepts which are designed by inquiry to resolve the special problems within the context in which they arise.

Dewey's basic thesis is that individuality develops—is actually made—through a process of interaction within social institutions. Criticizing the "individualistic schools" of the eighteenth and nineteenth centuries, Dewey writes:

---

* Ibid.
** John Dewey, *Human Nature and Conduct*, Henry Holt and Co., New York, 1922, pp. 315-332.

30

It based its individualism, philosophically speaking, upon the belief that individuals are alone real, that classes and organiza' tions are secondary and derived. They are artificial, while indi' viduals are natural. . . . The real difficulty is that the individual is regarded as something *given,* something already there. . . . Now it is true that social arrangements, laws, institutions are made for man, rather than that man is made for them; that they are means and agencies of human welfare and progress. But they are not means for obtaining something for individuals, not even happiness. They are means of *creating* individuals.*

Dewey is critical of all individual psychology which seeks an understanding of human nature in terms of an individual's traits, behavior patterns, dispositions, faculties, instincts, impulses, etc. For Dewey, this approach tends to obscure the basic fact that the individ' ual is essentially a process in the making, that human nature evolves within determinate social settings—the family, social habits and beliefs, and the whole range of social institutions—in which—first the child and later the adult functions as an individual and to which, in his varied quests for security and success, he must constantly accom' modate his entire being.

To understand the individual's formation by and dependence on the social group into which he is born and within which he lives out his destiny, it is essential to recognize the role of habit in human thought and conduct. "Man is a creature of habit, not of reason nor yet of instinct," and "[of] habits formed for the most part under the influence of the customs of the group."** The influence of habit is decisive because it forms the basis for all action and thought. The entire learning process aims at the formation of habit patterns, and the habits which we acquire spring from the customs and traditions of our culture.

Dewey is critical of those philosophical views which hold "that ideas and knowledge were functions of a mind or consciousness which originated in individuals by means of isolated contact with objects." In opposition to this, he insists that, "knowledge is a function of

---

* John Dewey, *Reconstruction in Philosophy,* Henry Holt and Company, New York, pp. 193-194.
** John Dewey, *Human Nature and Conduct,* p. 125.

association and communication; it depends upon tradition, upon tools and methods socially transmitted, developed and sanctioned."* He goes on to say that even "faculties of effectual observation, reflection and desire are habits acquired under the influence of the culture and institutions of society, not ready-made inherent powers."**

Thus, Dewey's thesis of the dependence of mind upon habit and of habit upon social conditions—a reconstruction of Hegelian thought —can be seen as the basic philosophical influence on current anthropological insights. Dewey's reliance on Hegel's "institutional idealism" is especially evident in his conception of freedom. While he is keenly aware of man's intricate involvement in and reliance on the institutions in his culture, he looks, as Hegel, to these same institutions for the attainment of human freedom. The individual advances his own freedom to the degree to which he participates not only in "the loyal maintenance of the existing institutions," but especially in their "idealization," their reorganization and reform. Dewey's conception of freedom rests on the interdependence of personal freedom with political and economic liberty. One cannot exist without the other. Unless our established institutions are transformed by conscientious citizens into dynamic agencies of political and economic liberty, individual freedom is impossible. In his essay on "Philosophies of Freedom," Dewey concludes as follows:

> I sum up by saying that the possibility of freedom is deeply grounded in our very beings. It is one with our individuality, our being uniquely what we are and not imitators and parasites of others. But like all other possibilities, this possibility has to be actualized; and, like all others, it can only be actualized through interaction with objective conditions. The question of political and economic freedom is not an addendum or afterthought, much less a deviation or excrescence, in the problem of personal freedom. For the conditions that form political and economic liberty are required in order to realize the potentiality of freedom each of us carries with him in his very structure.***

---

* John Dewey, *The Public and Its Problems*, Henry Holt and Co., New York, 1927, p. 158.

** *Ibid.*

*** John Dewey, *Philosophy and Civilization*, Minton, Balch and Co., New York, 1931, pp. 297-298.

One wonders why Dewey, who is fully cognizant of the dominance of our social institutions (he often speaks of the eclipse of the public in this technological age), continues to cling to the Hegelian tradition of institutionalized idealism when an overwhelming burden of evidence points to its obsolescence. Recent sociological findings demonstrate the emergence of a radically new type of democratic society in which political and economic institutions have been so transformed that the traditional view of their potential role in the life of the individual requires complete revision. Only a naive optimist will continue to view our social institutions today as the potential instruments for the attainment of personal freedom. A sober appraisal of their radically changed character in this era of mass democratization makes it clearly evident that, far from being potential builders of individuality and autonomy, our institutions have come to be, and will increasingly continue to be, the very deterrents of the freedom which earlier thinkers believed they were designed to promote. We have come to realize that the very institutions on which Dewey, as Hegel before him, relied for the actualization of personal freedom are, in actuality, the very forces which consciously inhibit, if not entirely crush, whatever tendencies the individual may already possess for the eventual creation of his personal freedom. Dewey himself, in his more sober moments, is highly skeptical of the possibility of "idealizing" social institutions into ultimate agencies of freedom. Critically reflecting on the spirit and the policies of our modern educational institutions, he writes:

> Even our deliberate education, our schools, are conducted so as to indoctrinate certain beliefs rather than to promote habits of thought. If that is true of them, what is not true of the other social institutions as to their effect upon thought?*

And he goes on:

> This state of things accounts, to my mind, for the current indifference to what is the very heart of actual freedom: freedom of thought. It is considered to be enough to have certain legal guarantees of its possibility. Encroachment upon the nom-

---

* *Ibid*, p. 296.

inal legal guarantees appears to arouse less and less resentment. Indeed, since the mere absence of legal restrictions may take effect only in stimulating the expression of half-baked and foolish ideas, and since the effect of their expression may be idle or harmful, popular sentiment seems to be growing less and less adverse to the exercise of even overt censorships.*

We have here a dual view of Dewey, one, the liberalist, the reformer, the idealist, who, by bent of temperament and philosophical preconceptions, is committed to the faith in the rationality of man, and in the ideal possibilities of social institutions, and the other, the realist, the critic, the skeptic who is profoundly disturbed over the indifference, the lethargy in public life today. Each of these two views of Dewey reflects a distinct cultural climate, the former a climate that is of another era—individualistic, optimistic, and rational —and the latter, a climate which has come to replace it—our current temper of deep skepticism, with its keen awareness of the irrationalities in our time. It is difficult to say which of the two Deweys makes this statement:

> I shall begin to believe that we care more for freedom than we do for imposing our own beliefs upon others in order to subject them to our will, when I see that the main purpose of our schools and other institutions is to develop powers of unremitting and discriminating observation and judgment.**

The cataclysm of events since this statement was written (the publication date is 1931) has enormously increased the disillusionment which made Dewey then doubt the capacity of rational men to "idealize" their social institutions, to infuse them with "powers of unremitting and discriminating observation and judgment." Ours is the era of mammoth organizations, of mass production, of standardization, and of centralization in government, setting the stage for the new mass society. With the huge economic and political systems—the huge trusts, the huge labor unions, the huge media of communication wielding public opinion—the field of responsibility and action left

---

* *Ibid,* pp. 296-297.
** *Ibid,* p. 297.

34

to the individual is so narrowed today that the political apathy which Dewey deplored is not likely to be lifted. In a few decades we have rapidly moved from the individualism of a restrictive liberal democracy to the mass civilization of today, where democracy is lodged in a government which has been pushed by its citizens to a measure of intervention and control where it is hardly distinguishable from its more totalitarian counterparts in socialist societies. We have learned, through bitter experience, that our democratic institutions, although theoretically grounded in liberty, are no less capable of inhibiting individual freedom than those in which the state is invested with arbitrary power over the lives of men. We have also come to learn that economic systems which are rooted in the tradition of free enterprise, laissez-faire, and rugged individualism can evolve into corporate industries producing an economic climate in which even the executive personnel of management is reduced to the "organization man."

Much has been written in recent years about the decline of reason and of respect for reason in human affairs. We have earlier referred to the revolutionary Freudian discoveries of the role of reason as a vehicle of "rationalization," of hidden motives and deep-seated attitudes. These Freudian discoveries have completely shattered the faith that men of intelligence and good will are likely, by process of rational discussion, to settle their differences and to reach correct opinions on controversial political questions. Perhaps this trust in reason was adequate in an age when such questions were relatively uncomplicated and when the educated layman required no specialized knowledge to deal with the political issues that challenged him to action. So long as the state was not required to intervene in economic issues and men could hope that by their political opinions and actions they could directly affect the shaping of political events, their faith in the power of reasoning to resolve their problems was not unwarranted. Today, political and economic matters are so complex and technical, that even the theorist is cautious in his analysis and prediction of socio-economic events. Without a staff of experts the layman is lost in coping with the complexities of the political and economic issues in this technological age. At the very top level of leadership there is constant reliance on a "brain-trust" for crucial decision-making. While the citizen is still made to believe that reason has not been dethroned from its supreme office of formulating policy, he is expected to subordinate his own reasoning to the superior wisdom of the expert.

In actuality, however, reason itself is deployed to undo reason. Political leaders are seen to use the rational findings of scientific investigation to promote their political views and objectives. From recent psychological and sociological findings they have learned that in this mass civilization men are more effectively moved by a subtle appeal to their emotions rather than by rational argumentation. The vehicle of indoctrination, they have discovered, works no less in the so-called free, democratic society than in the totalitarian state. Thus, propaganda has become as potent an instrument of mass democracy as advertising of the commodities of mass production. The political organizer today takes his cue from the commercial advertiser, selling the candidate to the voter by the same methods used to sell soap to the buying public. With the appeal no longer to reason, but to man's gullibility, political leaders consciously use irrational means to promote their own irrational ends—ends that are calculated not to promote the public good, but to advance the vested interests of powerful pressure-groups.

There are those who view the prevalent calculated use of the irrational techniques of persuasion—the molding and manipulation of public opinion by appeal to the irrational subconscious—as a new phenomenon of our technological age. They regard it as a peculiar affliction of the new mass democracy which has radically changed the role and function of our traditional institutions. Actually, the dominance of "unreason" or irrationality in the organized processes of society is, as we have seen, a significant insight of Hegel's philosophy of history. What is new is the diffusion of this insight as a result of the many sociological and psychological investigations which have come to corroborate what Hegel and other philosophers had recognized long before the advent of the Freudian discovery of the unconscious. What has happened is not the displacement of reason by a sudden insurgence of irrationality, but a keener, more wide-spread awareness of the subtler phases of reason as they operate beneath the surface of our consciousness as well as in the conscious sphere of "rationalization." What is required today is a careful philosophical analysis of the diverse operations of reason in the varied adjustmental processes of the individual in his society. The emphasis of such a study ought to be on a careful explication of reasoning as a vehicle of rationalization in contradistinction to reasoning in the moral sense. (We have made a beginning in this direction in Chapter 5, which deals with constructive, dynamic reason.)

We are today far more knowledgeable with regard to those effects upon human character which result from the individual's intricate involvement in the organized life of his society. Recent sociological studies, such as William H. Whyte's *The Organization Man* and David Riesman's *The Lonely Crowd,* and others, have given us a substantive body of information in this area. These investigations shed a great deal of light on the subtle pressures, conflicts, tensions, and even neuroses, especially of the men in the upper management level in the big corporate organizations of industry. There is general agreement, based on impressive evidence, that involvement in large organizations today inhibits those personality traits which go into the making of human freedom. In fact, there is a direct correlation between the degree of involvement and the measure of suppression of personal freedom. The more involved men become within corporate institutions, the more they tend to surrender their independence of judgment and outlook. Advancement within the organization requires complete identification with it; to secure promotion is to make the organization's interests and goals synonymous with one's own. While the "organization man" chafes at the pressures to conformity, he finds it impossible to resist their corrosive effects.

Whyte finds that even the industrial elite—the decision-making body of economic institutions—is helpless in the face of the organization's crushing impact on the individual's drive to autonomy. In conflicts between the desire "to control one's own destiny" and the pressure to submergence within the larger group, freedom is inevitably victimized. In Whyte's own words:

> The real conflict . . . is the conflict within work. Of all the organization men, the true executive is the one who remains most suspicious of the Organization. If there is one thing that characterizes him, it is a fierce desire to control his own destiny and, deep down, he resents yielding that control to the Organ-

ization, no matter how velvety its grip. He does not want to be done right by; he wants to dominate, not be dominated.

But he can't act that way. He must not only accept control, he must accept it as if he liked it. He must smile when he is transferred to a place or job that isn't the job or place he happens to want. He must appear to enjoy listening sympathetically to points of view not his own. He must be less "goal-centered," more "employee-centered." It is not enough now that he work hard; he must be a damn good fellow to boot.*

Current findings indicate that the growing pressures upon the dynamic personality within the gigantic corporate structures are so alarming that the incidence of executive neuroses has become a widespread phenomenon. While the people from the great reaches of middle management can easily accommodate themselves to the pressures to conformity because they basically seek integration within the group (their sense of belongingness and dependence is far stronger than the tendency to autonomy), the dynamic men on the top incur deep neurotic complexes as the result of their conflict between autonomy and the organization's demand for integration within the system. In fact, there is evidence of a new philosophy of economic creativity which makes team work, collective thinking, the key to invention, research and discovery. Viewing the group as a creative vehicle, the Organization deliberately coerces its scientists into the framework of cooperative dynamics to such a degree that our progressive economists have come to view it as a real menace to our country's economic growth.

In an article on "Strengthening Free Institutions in the United States," John Jewkes describes the problem as follows:

When the contributions of individuals tend to be belittled or ignored and exaggerated claims are made for the virtues of team work; when change is frowned upon unless it can be introduced in a neat and tidy way; when the short period pains of readjustments are unduly magnified and longer period benefits discounted; when institutions are allowed to be both advocate

---

* William H. Whyte, *The Organization Man*, Doubleday Anchor Book, New York, 1956, pp. 166-167.

and judge of their own cause; when the responsibility for making decisions, or failing to make them, can be so deeply buried within a hierarchical organization that no one can ever be held to be individually responsible for anything—in all such cases we know we are in the presence of something which is destructive of growth.*

Jewkes deplores the fact that little "seems to be heard of the crucial need to provide room for the individual inventor, the freelance technologist, the uncommitted scientist." While he regards the provision for individual creativity in today's economy "to be one of the requisite foundations for economic growth," he fails to tell us how this challenge is to be met.

Whyte reports that the prevalent response to the challenge of individualism is best reflected in the advice of one company president given to a group of aspiring young executives, "that the ideal is to be an individualist privately and a conformist publicly." This may be an "ideal" for one who has himself yielded to the pressure to conformity, but viewed from the perspective of the ethical agent this surrender of autonomy in the face of outer dominance is, as will be seen, decidedly unethical. The reasoning of the company president is a typical example of "rationalizing away" one's inability to *resist* one's culture's dominant pressures. It is precisely here, in the conflict between *cultural deterrents to personal freedom* and the inner urge to self-determination where we encounter a crucial ethical choice. Whether or not we meet this challenge may well determine the destiny of freedom in our time. Unless men and women in our generation and in generations to come become cognizant of the challenge, ethics itself can hope to be of no more than a purely academic import.

With more and more Americans huddling for security in group belongingness, it is utterly illusory to expect new thought-patterns to bring about a reversal of the frightful retreat of individualism. Such self-delusion is apparent in the studies of Riesman and others, especially in their discussion of the possible ways in which a more autonomous type of social character might develop in the industrial

---

* John Jewkes, *Problems of United States Economic Development*, Vol. 1, January, 1958, Published by The Committee for Economic Development 711 Fifth Ave., New York 22, N. Y.

age. Riesman's analysis, in *The Lonely Crowd,* of today's pervasive character structure is a forceful demonstration of the submergence of individuality and independence of outlook and conviction where approval of one's peer group is found to be the dominant motivation of human conduct. In the final part of the work, titled "Autonomy," Riesman and his colleagues anticipate the possible emergence of a new type of characterology, in which men and women of tomorrow are optimistically seen to emancipate themselves from today's pressures to conformity. This is to be the consequence of an increasing disorganization, i.e., a disintegration of class stratification—the byproducts of the complexities of our technological age. Riesman and his colleagues pin their hopes for the emergence of autonomous character on "creative utopian thinking." "In the end," they write, "our few suggestions are paltry ones, and we can only conclude our discussion by saying that a vastly greater stream of creative utopian thinking is needed before we can see more clearly the goal we dimly suggest by the word "autonomy."*

Obviously, these sociologists reflect their own inner doubts when they go on to say that "The reader who recalls our beginnings with the large, blind movements of population growth and economic and technological change may ask whether we seriously expect utopian thinking, no matter how inspired, to counter whatever fate for men these movements have in store."** But despite the keenest awareness of the "intractabilities and self-reproducing tendencies of character," as well as the "massed obstacles to change inherent in social structure and character structure," these sociologists believe that mere "ideas" can bring about a real alteration of deeply entrenched attitudes and beliefs.

What we have here is a manifestation of the irrational in the so-called rational man: the theorist's refusal to surrender an obsolete, naive faith in the power of reason to effect serious changes in culturally determined patterns of behavior.

Unless we begin to take seriously the insights of philosophers like Hegel and Spinoza, we shall fail to comprehend the "crises of irrationality" in our time. We must learn from Hegel that the operations

---

* David Riesman, Nathan Glazer, Reuel Denney, *The Lonely Crowd,* Doubleday and Co., Inc., Garden City, New York, 1954, p. 346.
** *Ibid,* p. 347.

of men in their society are under the dominion of "unreason," and that unless, like Hegel, we put our trust in a transcending Absolute Spirit which somehow can make irrationality the instrumentality of an eventual self-realization of reason, unless we are willing to accept such "peculiar" metaphysics, we cannot hope that by the sheer power of human reason we can move an attitude of irrationality. This writer, for one, refuses to pin his hope on some transcendent Absolute Reason to meet a challenge with which we here on earth must grapple lest we abandon our faith in sanity altogether.

If we cannot trust reason to accomplish the task, what possible alternative is there? We must take our cue from Spinoza who teaches us that emotionally rooted attitudes can be countered and replaced only by stronger opposing emotional attitudes. We reiterate that to overcome the force of passion, one must mobilize the *resistance* of a passional counter force. Mere ideas, however, inspired, are powerless to do this.

We have seen in our generation dramatic evidence of the power of resistance to the encroachments on human freedom. The many underground movements in the lands under Nazi tyranny are testimony to the capacity of man to oppose the force of oppression once his emotions are sufficiently roused to resist the aggressor. The Negro revolution in our country is living proof of Spinoza's thesis that entrenched emotive attitudes can be replaced only by stirring opposing emotional attitudes into a militant counter offensive. Were it not for the momentum of mass demonstrations, in which not only the age-old apathy of the Negro population has been transformed into deep resentment, but in which the indifference of the "well-intentioned" non-Negro has been shaken, the present climate of militant resistance would not have come into being.

The Negro leaders today are wise to reject the counsel of patience, to refuse to put their trust in a gradual evolution of their rights. They are wise to rebuff the counsel of "reason" at this stage in their revolution, because the experience of a century has demonstrated to them that reliance on the so-called reasonable man for redress of their grievances is futile. There is no doubt that the recent passing of the Civil Rights Bill in Congress is the consummate effect of the Negro's impassioned resistance against age-old indignities, of his militant policy of non-violent civil disobedience.

The Negro's revolutionary anthem, "We shall overcome," is a mighty motivational force in stirring the human passion for freedom into active resistance. The Negro's march for freedom, powered as it is by deep emotions, has profound moral implications. Not only is it an inspiration in the battle of resistance against dominant pressures in all areas of life, but it has a significant lesson for ethics today.

Ethical ideas are impotent as guides to moral action so long as they are not reinforced by powerful emotionally-charged attitudes. So long as we find emotional security in conforming to the cultural patterns of our time, so long will we remain fettered by their hold on us. An awakening can come only through sober honest introspection by the individual himself, by focussing on the ugly manifestations of his conformity—the tensions and conflicts that he suffers in surrendering the control over his destiny to powerful pressures from without, be they economical or political or social in character.

The dynamic men in our culture—and it is on these alone that we can rely for tomorrow's emergence of autonomy or personal freedom—must not only resent the pressure to conformity (which in accordance with all indications they indeed do), but must make this resentment a powerful, passional counter force against the "secondary gains" of conformity. They must come to realize that in the long run the gains are, by far, outweighed by the losses in the battle for human freedom which will ultimately determine all human destiny.

There are many battlegrounds on which we are made to believe, or make ourselves believe, that the cause we are fighting for is freedom. However, there is but one battleground on which we can make certain that in the fight for freedom we are not the victims of indoctrination by seduction from without or delusion from within. This single battleground is the individual's own life in all its interrelations: the family, in which the deepest needs are more frustrated than fulfilled; the organizations, in which the highest aspirations are more blocked than advanced; the government, in which the noblest loyalties are more abused than inspired. All these areas of an individual's life, interlaced and interdependent as they are, constitute a total organism, one unitary field of battle. In it there can be no partial victory for freedom; it is either wholly won or entirely lost.

Compromise with freedom in any of these areas leads inevitably to final surrender of one's individuality, independence, self-respect, the very dignity of man. There is but one genuine loyalty, the loyalty to one's own freedom. This loyalty must exceed all others. Ironically, Shakespeare's words: "This above all to thine own self be true . . . thou canst not then be false to any man," has taken on the hollow ring of a worn cliché, but we may well invoke it in this context.

Unless the desire for self-expression, independence, autonomy and self-determination becomes a passion at least as great as any other, we cannot possibly hope to attain the freedom which, in a democratic society, is held to be the foundation of the good life. A realistic appraisal of the character of our social institutions in this new age of mass democratization must sober us to the realization that it is no longer feasible to hope that by *individual* efforts we can transform them into bastions of freedom. Today we can no longer speak of free societies or free institutions in the proper sense. Far from securing freedom, they diminish it the moment the individual relaxes his guard against the constant invasion into the limited areas of personal independence which are still open to him. We must begin to recognize that, in actuality, the real threat to our freedom is the bigness of corporate institutions, be they economic or social or political.

The attainment of freedom can be secured by none but the individual himself. It consists, in its initial stage, in a powerful resistance against the dominance of social institutions, against the molding forces inherent in one's culture. So far from fulfilling himself within organized society (as Hegel and his followers, E. Durkheim at the turn of the century, or Dewey later, or the school of Mayo and Warner today, would have us believe), the individual today is inhibited, if not crushed, by it in his quest for autonomy.

While we cannot help being involved in many organizations, we need not make involvement within any organization a total one. It becomes imperative, as Clark Kerr, Chancellor of the University of California at Berkeley, has urged, "to seek to whatever extent lies within [one's] power, to limit each group to the minimum control necessary for performance of essential functions. . . ."*

---

* Quoted in *The Organization Man*, p. 51.

Thus, resistance to cultural determinations calls for a philosophy of *non-involvement*, for the cultivation of the Stoic's attitude of detachment, where we lend our energies to many organizations and give ourselves to none. Rather, we must give ourselves to the life task of self-fulfillment, the fashioning of character into a dynamic, autonomous personality structure—the ethical man.

CHAPTER THREE

Psychological Deterrents
to Freedom

THE CULTURAL DETERRENTS to human freedom have a powerful
ally in certain psychological drives, the satisfaction of which makes
most men and women dependent upon some organized form of activity.
The impulse to power, the quest for fame or glory, the drive for
recognition, the hunger for sex, the need for security, the fear of
loneliness—these are the dominant psychological forces which can
draw us almost irresistibly into deep involvement in and slavish dependence upon our social institutions. The more we yield to the
pull of these forces, the more difficult it becomes to attain human
freedom. When we add to these the unconscious forces which, as
recent clinical psychology has shown, determine not only much of our
overt conduct, but also desire, judgment, belief and idealization, we
see the goal of personal freedom extend beyond the range of possible
human attainment. We need not here enter into the debate whether
or not there is a single basic drive to which all others are reducible.
Whether it is Hobbes' quest for power, or Freud's sex drive, or Adler's
striving for superiority, each can become so dominant as to chain us
to "human bondage." The psychological deterrents to human freedom,
those which drive us into diverse social entanglements, constitute another set of obstacles which men must somehow overcome if they seek
mastery over their own destiny.

While much of our psychological dynamism pulls us into group-
directed interactions of one kind or another, *we are not by native
endowment, committed to belongingness within a group.* This is borne
out by current insights in genetics. In his essay, "Eugenics and Society," Julian Huxley stresses the point that genetically there are

tendencies to both social and anti-social action. "There is no doubt," he writes, "that genetic differences of temperament, including tendencies to social or anti-social action, to co-operation or individualism, do exist, nor that they could be bred for in man as man has bred for tameness and other temperamental traits in many domestic animals; . . ."* Huxley's program of social planning reflects the tradition which is committed to the thesis (described above) that men can fulfill themselves only *within society,* by effective adjustment to the environing patterns of thought and behavior. This is especially evident from his counsel "to raise the power of group incentives" and "to frame eugenic measures for encouraging the spread of genes for social virtues."** While Huxley calls for a social environment which gives "satisfaction to the possessors of social traits such as altruism, readiness to co-operate, sensitiveness, sympathetic enthusiasm, and so forth, instead of, as now, putting a premium on many anti-social traits such as egoism, low cunning, insensitiveness, and ruthless concentration,"*** the demand for human freedom today calls for a social environment radically different from the one which Huxley regards as desirable. In fact, Huxley is seen to "idealize" the very traits which make for today's conformity and submergence within the group. To advance the cause of human freedom, it is imperative that we encourage those traits and tendencies which, from Huxley's point of vantage may be taken as anti-social, but which, from the vantage point of the ethical agent, may be better described as conducive to individuality, self-reliance and self-determination.

Ruth Benedict, in *Patterns of Culture,* makes it quite clear that the recognition of the wide diversity of cultures no longer warrants the classification of human traits in terms of rigid, universally applicable categories:

> The diversity of cultures can be endlessly documented. A field of human behavior may be ignored in some societies until it barely exists; it may even be in some cases unimagined. Or it

---

* Julian Huxley, *Man in the Modern World,* The New American Library, New York, 1944, p. 57.
** *Ibid.*
*** *Ibid,* p. 56.

46

may almost monopolize the whole organized behavior of the society, and the most alien situation be manipulated only in its terms. Traits having no intrinsic relation one with the other, and historically independent, merge and become inextricable, providing the occasion for behavior that has no counterpart in regions that do not make these identifications. It is a corollary of this that standards, no matter in what aspect of behavior, range in different cultures from the positive to the negative pole.*

From all this it follows that, in reply to Mr. Huxley, we may say that what is taken to be social in one culture may be regarded as anti-social in another culture. "Social virtues" are relative to the culture and its peculiar patterns of conduct and thought. Since free-dom is basic and indispensable, not only for the fulfillment of the individual, but also for the maintenance of our democratic institu-tions, we must value and seek to cultivate those traits in our society that make for free individuals—the sole guarantors of our democratic institutions. In accordance with anthropological findings, it is not at all a utopian objective to propose the cultivation of character traits which make for autonomy, such as open-mindedness, independence of judgment and belief, self-reliance, initiative, intellectual curiosity, creativeness, etc. Professor Benedict insists that "man is not com-mitted in detail by his biological constitution to any particular variety of behavior."** She goes on to say that "the great diversity of social solutions that man has worked out in different cultures . . . are all equally possible on the basis of his original endowment."*** While it is true that we are determined by our psychological constitution, it is unwarranted to infer that this determination makes human free-dom impossible. There are psychological traits which inhibit freedom and there are psychological traits which make for freedom. It is im-portant that we distinguish between *dynamic* character traits, which are describable as *self-determining,* and those character traits which must be seen to be *psychologically determined.* While the former enable the individual to have control over his actions, the latter per-

---

* Ruth Benedict, *Patterns of Culture,* p. 52.
** *Ibid,* p. 27.
*** *Ibid.*

mit of no such control, especially in crucial decision-making. (We shall elaborate upon this in Chapter 4 which deals with the diverse processes of character formation.)

The prevalence of a given set of character traits in a culture, or, in other words, its typical characterology, is, to a large extent, dependent upon that culture's dominant purposes and values. "In obedience to these purposes," Prof. Benedict writes, "each people further and further consolidates its experience, and in proportion to the urgency of these drives the heterogeneous items of behaviour take more and more congruous shape. Taken up by a well-integrated culture, the most ill-assorted acts become characteristic of its peculiar goals, often by the most unlikely metamorphoses. The form that these acts take we can understand only by understanding first the emotional and intellectual mainsprings of that society."*

What are the over-riding purposes of our culture? Are they favorable to the cultivation of dynamic, self-determining character traits? Prof. Benedict gives us frank and convincing answers to both these questions, and the answers frame an ugly picture of our American culture, a picture strongly confirmed by recent sociological studies. Prof. Benedict's characterization of our culture's paramount purposes: 1. the "amassing of private possessions" and 2. the "multiplication of the occasions of display"** (Veblen's "conspicuous consumption") is further documented in such works as *The Acquisitive Society*, by R. Tawney, and *The Status Seekers*, by V. Packard.

Prof. Benedict attributes to these dominant purposes the prevalent exploitation of children by parents who, far from respecting the individual rights of the young, make them extensions of their own egos, supplying "special opportunity for the display of authority."

> Without the clue that in our civilization at large man's paramount aim is to amass private possessions and multiply occasions of display, the modern position of the wife and the modern emotions of jealousy are alike unintelligible. Our attitudes toward our children are equally evidences of this same cultural goal. Our children are not individuals whose rights and tastes are casually respected from infancy, as they are in some primi-

---

* *Ibid*, p. 53.
** *Ibid*.

tive societies, but special responsibilities, like our possessions, to which we succumb or in which we glory, as the case may be. They are fundamentally extensions of our own egos and give a special opportunity for the display of authority. The pattern is not inherent in the parent-children situations, as we so glibly assume. It is impressed upon the situation by the major drives of our culture, and it is only one of the occasions in which we follow our traditional obsessions.*

Prof. Benedict readily acknowledges the deep influence which John Dewey has had on her ideas. One recognizes this influence not only in her analysis of the plasticity of native impulses, but also in her critique of prevalent parent-child relations. John Dewey has given us a scathing indictment of the exploitation, by the adult generation, of the infant child's plastic malleable impulses for the preservation of our nature's established traditions.

But for the most part adults have given training rather than education. An impatient, premature mechanization of impulsive activity after the fixed pattern of adult habits of thought and affection has been desired. The combined effect of love of power, timidity in the face of the novel and a self-admiring complacency has been too strong to permit immature impulse to exercise its reorganizing potentialities. The younger generation has hardly even knocked frankly at the door of adult customs, much less been invited in to rectify through better education the brutalities and iniquities established in adult habits. Each new generation has crept blindly and furtively through such chance gaps as have happened to be left open. Otherwise it has been modeled after the old.**

John Dewey's analysis of the potential role of our native psychological stock reinforces our contention that the cultivation of autonomous character traits is far from a utopian ideal. In critical reaction to those psychological theories which ground human behavior in fixed, determinate, basic drives, John Dewey insists that the impulses of

---

* *Ibid,* p. 213.
** John Dewey, *Human Nature and Conduct,* pp. 96-97.

the child are inchoate and exceedingly flexible, capable of being shaped by their social environment into whatever patterns of behavior or character traits are desired by that environment.

> Yet it goes without saying that original, unlearned activity has its distinctive place and that an important one in conduct. Impulses are the pivots upon which the re-organization of activities turn, they are agencies of deviation, for giving new directions to old habits and changing their quality. Consequently whenever we are concerned with understanding social transition and flux or with projects for reform, personal and collective, our study must go to analysis of native tendencies.*

Our homes and our schools have it within their power to mold our children either into docile conforming adults, or into free self-determining individuals. Shall we perpetuate our present cultural "image," or shall we lay the foundations for a *real* free society in which the dynamic, self-reliant, autonomous personality—our culture's "idealized" character structure—is realized in our future way of life? While this is a realistic challenge, it is clear from all indications that we fail to meet it. Nor shall we meet it in the future if current trends continue to prevail. As has been pointed out before, it is illusory to expect our social institutions, especially our homes and our schools, to reverse the current trend to collectivism. So far from being builders of autonomous character, they are the very breeding grounds of docility and conformity in our children.

Riesman's findings demonstrate that social approbation has become the dominant incentive in the American home.

> Approval itself, irrespective of content, becomes almost the only unequivocal good in this situation: one makes good when one is approved of. Thus all power, not merely some power, is in the hands of the actual or imaginary approving group, and the child learns from his parents' reactions to him that nothing in his character, no possession he owns, no inheritance of name or talent, no work he has done is valued for itself but only for its

---

* *Ibid,* pp. 92-93.

effect on others. Making good becomes almost equivalent to making friends, or at any rate the right kind of friends. "To him that hath approval, shall be given more approval."*

Today's pervasive trend of "other-directedness" confronts the individual parent with a crucial ethical choice: shall he yield to dominant trends and like most parents in the peer group inculcate in his child the sense of approbation as an incentive of conduct, or shall he *resist* it and develop his child's tendencies to autonomy and independence? Of course, parents are not likely to decide in favor of autonomy, so long as they themselves are culturally conditioned to "other-directedness." Dewey frames the moral issue in similar terms:

> The moral problem in child and adult alike as regards impulse and instinct is to utilize them for formation of new habits, or what is the same thing, the modification of an old habit so that it may be adequately serviceable under novel conditions.**

This moral problem is one which a parent must resolve in his own individual home. It is a problem which we must meet as individuals, rather than expect to have it resolved collectively. It would be self-delusion on the part of parents to look to our present schools for the building of autonomous character structure. The fact is that the impress of "other directedness" has made serious inroads into our educational institutions, especially on the level of our public schools, entrusted as they are with the task of forming the character of our younger generation. Riesman shows that in consequence of our culture's "other-directed socialization," our schools manifest a serious reaction to yesterday's tenets of progressive education. Today's alleged progressive education is, in actuality, no longer progressive. Far from developing the individuality of the child, our schools tend to thwart it. The role of the teacher has been recast from builder of individuality to that of "opinion leader:"

> The teacher's role in this situation is often that of opinion leader. She is the one who spreads the message concerning taste

---

* Riesman, *The Lonely Crowd*, p. 66.
** Dewey, *Human Nature and Conduct*, p. 104.

51

that comes from the progressive urban centers. She conveys to the children that what matters is not their industry of learning as such but their adjustment to the group, their cooperation, their (carefully stylized and limited) initiative and leadership.*

In placing the responsibility of building autonomous character with the *individual* parent, we are particularly mindful of Dewey's counsel that "a valid moral theory contrasts with all those theories which set up static goals, (even when they are called perfection), and with those theories which idealize raw impulse and find in its spontaneities an adequate mode of human freedom."** This individualistic ethical theory, grounded as it is in the ethical agent, entrusts the attainment of freedom neither to our native endowment, nor to future evolutionary developments to which certain ethical writers like Spencer have looked, nor to supernatural metaphysical agencies, nor even to God. This individualistic theory relies, for the attainment of human freedom, on the ethical agent alone. Unless there are, in fact, ethical agents who secure, by their own efforts, individual freedom, the domain of freedom is simply non-existent.

A thinker who denies that freedom exists is generally regarded as an extreme skeptic. Current findings in the social sciences demonstrate that the skeptic's view of freedom is indeed close to the truth, that what has been regarded as extreme skepticism is, in actuality, a sober realistic appraisal of the state of human freedom today. To appreciate how extremely narrow the actual boundaries of freedom are today, we must have a clear conception of the present climate of our social institutions.

If we are interested in human behavior, we need first of all to understand the institutions that are provided in any society. For human behaviour will take the forms those institutions suggest, even to extremes of which the observer, deep-dyed in the culture of which he is a part, can have no intimation.***

It may well be that only the trained anthropologist can be expected to achieve the kind of detachment which would enable one

---

* Riesman, *The Lonely Crowd*, p. 83.
** Dewey, *Human Nature and Conduct*, p. 105.
*** Ruth Benedict, *Patterns of Culture*, pp. 206-207.

to view one's own culture with the same objectivity with which one might possibly view another culture. Nevertheless, an objective observer can do no less than acknowledge that what is anthropologically valid in respect to cultures in general, applies with equal force to one's own culture in particular. Nothing less can be expected of the ethical agent. Unless we achieve this kind of detachment, we cannot be sure whether we are entirely free from the determinations of our culture or the psychological compulsions which bind us to it.

To become an ethical agent, we must acquire not only self-knowledge, a knowledge of the dominant traits in our own character, but also a knowledge of our culture, its dominant traits as well as its overriding purposes.* We must understand that they are compulsive, not in proportion as they are basic and essential to human behavior, but in the degree to which they are pervasive and dominant within our culture. We must understand the enormous malleability of our native endowment. While this important aspect of human nature tends to make the great mass of individuals susceptive to the characteristic traits and forms in their social environment, there are always those who, by virtue of peculiar circumstance or differentiated background, are plastic to influences and molding forces which make for autonomous, inner-directed patterns of thought and conduct. These are our potential ethical agents. Numerically they are negligible indeed, but qualitatively they give us our prophets, our rebels, our innovators in every clime and epoch. One may argue that this limits enormously not only the ranks of ethical agents, but also the actual sphere of ethical performances. But experience proves again and again that while most people avow a moral code, they fail to adhere to it in practice, especially when job security or other vital interests are at stake.

An ethical theory, if it is to be adequate, must take account of the basic fact that the ethical agent is as rare as it is difficult to *resist* dominant pressures from without and psychological determinations from within. It is especially difficult to mobilize resistance against these two kinds of deterrents to freedom, because they tend to reinforce one another to such a degree that only the possessor of a

---

* See Below, Chapter 5, pp. 7-13.

53

dynamic character structure—however he may have come to it—will be able to achieve it.

The trouble with most ethical theories is that they have failed to do justice to the basic fact that resistance to dominant pressures is an indispensable prerequisite of personal freedom.

Take, for example, the Hedonists who make pleasure the criterion and the goal of ethical behavior. They tend to ignore the fact that the quest for pleasure is likely to make of the individual a victim of compulsive inner drives where the true reasons of his conduct are covered up by rationalization. The quest for pleasure, far from mobilizing resistance to determinations from within and/or without, tends to break it down or to inhibit it from ever coming into being.

Or, take the Absolutists who look to a transcendent authority for the sanction of universal ethical values. They tend to subordinate the factor of resistance to outer control to the principle of adherence to law. Theological absolutist systems have gone so far as to hypostatize submissiveness to the deity into the supreme virtue of self-effacement. The absolutist plays directly into the hands of totalitarian forms of ideology. It is not historical coincidence that totalitarian systems of government have sprung up predominantly in countries where absolutist theological creeds prevailed. It is, therefore, futile to speculate about the prospect of future underground resistance in these totalitarian states. When people have been conditioned to allegiance to some higher authority, they are not likely to mobilize resistance when one form of authority is displaced by another.

Perhaps this accounts, in the deepest sense, for the tragedy of Nazi Germany, in which loyalty to the Fuehrer became the supreme moral principle. The Germanic idealization of duty and obedience, which not even the spirit of the Weimar Republic could dislodge, provided fertile ground for the horrendous Nazi morality. One need not wonder at the total absence of any tangible resistance to Nazi tyranny within the Third Reich.

A moral system in which obedience to law is the prime motivation of ethical conduct is not likely to give us energetic proponents of autonomy or self-determination. On the contrary, such systems are the least immune to rationalizations which cloak one's inability to resist domination from within and/or without in the garb of pseudo-ethical convictions.

With freedom as the indispensable foundation of ethics, it becomes imperative that we root the source and sanction of ethical values in such a manner that the autonomy or self-determination of the ethical agent is rendered secure. Ethical writers must guard against the danger of courting the rationalizing tendencies in our psychological make-up which make us so readily surrender autonomy to some higher outside power.

Once we recognize that resistance to cultural and psychological determinations is a prime requisite of personal freedom, it becomes evident that the determination of ethical principles and goals must be left entirely to the ethical agent. Otherwise he cannot be expected to be free, to be autonomous and self-determining, especially in moments of crucial ethical choices. The ethical agent cannot be required to entrust the determination of what is right or wrong to any authority than his own, be that authority grounded in the morality of his society, or in an alleged universal reign of law, or even in God. If the ethical agent is to be responsible for his moral conduct, he must be free not only to choose moral precepts, but also to determine whether or not a given precept or law is indeed an ethical one. If we seek to secure autonomy and self-determination, we can do no other than root the source and sanction of ethical values in the ethical agent himself. Only by so doing can we make certain that the foundations of freedom are firmly established.

Thus, it becomes evident that one of the basic implications of the primacy of the ethical agent is the relativity of ethical norms and goals. One readily recognizes that, unlike other relativist theories, our ethical relativism is not derived from anthropological conclusions. While we cannot deny the wide diversity of cultural customs and mores, it is unwarranted to infer from the *existence* of different moralities that ethical values *ought to differ* from culture to culture. The existence of diverse moral habits and beliefs is no proof of ethical relativism. It may well be that a careful examination of the different cultural mores will reveal certain basic universal standards and goals which underlie them all. To reduce the determination of ethical values to non-ethical considerations—to reduce what *ought to be* to *what is*—or to abstract ethical norms and goals from anthropological data, is to lose sight of G. E. Moore's demonstration of the uniqueness of the ethical in experience. We shall show at a later stage that the recognition of the primacy of the ethical agent sheds new light on the uniqueness of ethical values. For the present, it is essential that we distinguish between sociological relativism and ethical relativism. Sociological relativism is the recognition that moral habits and beliefs not only differ from culture to culture, but also that they are relative to its dominant needs and purposes, and that historically they tend to change with the evolving economic and political realities. Ethical relativism is the insistence that ethical values are relative to the ethical agent—his own long run needs, interests and life goals.

While ethical relativism flows from the primacy of the ethical agent, it derives added impetus from the recognition of the futility of universal ethical values. Kant's attempt at establishing universality in ethics demonstrates not only that this tends to make ethical maxims inapplicable to the concrete specific problems of ordinary experience, but also that it requires recourse to metaphysical categories which transcend the existential domain of the ethical agent. It is not unlikely, as we have stated before, that Kant's quest for universality in ethics is basically motivated by the scientific preconceptions of his time, that his belief in the universal reign of ethical laws is inspired by the Newtonian conception of the universal and absolute laws of motion. It is today a commonplace assertion that the classical scientific view of universal and absolute laws in nature has become untenable in the light of the new theories of relativity. That scientific concepts and theories must be taken as tentative and hypothetical, subject to revision in the light of new scientific discovery, is so fundamental to science today that a return to absolutism is utterly unlikely.

Absolutism in ethics is untenable, not only because it lodges ultimate authority outside of the ethical agent, but also because it tends toward dogmatism and inflexible adherence to one's beliefs and judgments. Ethical relativism, on the other hand, makes for open-mindedness and respect for the values and moral attitudes of others. It has always been a primary concern of moral philosophers, not only to frame a system of good life, but also to minimize conflict, to resolve opposing moral claims by argumentation rather than by force, to foster peaceable human relations wherever possible. Absolutist moralities, so far from minimizing the use of force to settle moral conflicts, can be and constantly have been used to justify it. It is no accident that religious persecutions have been predominantly perpetrated in the name of some absolutist moral creed. Because of his commitment to an "infallible universal truth," the absolutist is, in practice, far more likely to become embroiled in irreconcilable moral conflicts. He finds it impossible to comprehend why his opponent fails to "see the light" and inevitably attributes a denial of his "truths" to obstinacy or moral deficiency.

The relativist's commitment to his values and judgments is of an entirely different nature. Not only is he aware that his ethical values and moral judgments are relevant only to his own moral situation, but he is ready to acknowledge possible error in his reasoning. Insisting on his own freedom in moral decisions, he is far more likely to respect the freedom of another to make moral claims of his own. We shall show that a proper understanding of the ethical agent's freedom implies respect for another's freedom. In case of conflicting moral claims, ethical relativists will find it in keeping with their ethics to resolve their moral differences in a peaceable manner.

A theory of ethical relativism derived from the primacy of the ethical agent does not necessarily imply a subjectivist conception of ethical values and judgments. To assert that ethical choices are relevant to the ethical agent's long-range interests and goals is not to make them arbitrary or dependent upon the caprice of the individual. Nor does it mean, as logical empiricists maintain, that ethical judgments are non-cognitive, that they are necessarily matters of emotional preference or taste. Taking our stand with the philosophical principle of objective relativism, we shall seek to show that ethical values can be both relative and objective. Objective relativism basically means that a quality or property is an objective constituent in an organic whole, even though its existence depends on the relations in which it stands to other organic aspects, or to the whole. To adapt this principle to ethical matters we must create conditions which will enable the ethical agent to make the data which are relevant to him an appropriate basis for warranted knowledge claims.

One thing is clear—to deny the possibility of knowledge or rational opinion in ethics, and to doubt whether we can give good reasons for doing this rather than that, is an utterly intolerable position to one who refuses to ground crucial moral decisions on the quicksand of pure emotionality. The basic failure of both subjectivists and objectivists is that they have made the nature and purpose of moral judgments unintelligible by the attempt to elucidate them by means of a logical apparatus unsuited to the purpose. Reliance on analogies from the sciences for the elucidation of the objective character of ethics has proven unenlightening. We cannot expect objectivity in ethics to be analogous to what is taken to be objective in the empirical data of the sciences. The realm of ethical values and the realm of empirical matters of fact are incommensurate; one cannot be judged by the other. The incommensurability of these two disparate realms becomes clearly evident when the distinction between them is made from the perspective of the ethical agent. That ethical data are uniquely distinct from those of the sciences is fairly obvious. Whereas the data with which scientists deal are public data, available to any qualified investigator who makes the appropriate observations, the data of ethics are initially private data, accessible only to the ethical agent to whom they are relevant. The reasoning processes of an ethical agent, it will be seen, are uniquely distinct from those of the scientist. This does not necessarily mean that ethical data are immune to objective valuation and warranted knowledge claims. What is required is a careful distinction between the type of reasoning involved in scientific discovery and the type of reasoning by which the ethical agent is enabled to make adequate value judgments in the resolution of crucial moral choices. (These are the major objectives of Chapter 5.) Although ethical data consist of the ethical agent's own motives, purposes, goals, alternate courses of action, etc., the ethical agent, if equipped with proper criteria, can make these data the basis for objective valuation.

To establish ethics on objective grounds, we do not require a system of universal norms and goals. Nor need we rely, as Prichard and other objectivists, on the dubious support of intuition for the apprehension of the objective aspects of an ethical situation. What is needed, instead, is a set of criteria which will enable the ethical agent to make valid value judgments, to determine objectively whether or not a given act or norm or goal is an ethical one. These criteria flow logically from the very concept of the ethical agent. Provisionally, we may define an ethical agent as a "personality" who lives by and is committed to freedom in a dual aspect; freedom *from* inner compulsion and outer domination, and freedom *for* a constructive,

58

self-designed, self-reliant, and self-determined way of life. The ethical agent is one who is both the creator and the master of a unique individuality of his own. His freedom to make ethical choices is limited only by the freedom of another human being. This is in keeping with Kant's principle that "humanity and every rational nature is an end in itself (*which is the supreme limiting condition of the freedom of the action of every single person*)."* The freedom of another, as the limiting condition of the ethical agent's own freedom, is consistent with our two-fold conception of freedom. The obligation to respect another's freedom is not an "ought" which requires special justification. It is logically implied in the definition of the ethical agent. A person who infringes upon the freedom of another, either by imposing his will or power upon another human being or by advancing his own interest to the injury of another, demonstrates by so doing that he himself is not entirely free. Infringement upon the freedom of another is a clear indication of a deficiency in one's own freedom. Only he is free who relies entirely upon his own resources for the satisfaction of his needs and the realization of his goals. The need to dominate others or to use others as tools for self-aggrandizement springs from weakness rather than from strength, from insecurity rather than inner security. The quest for dominion over other human beings is psychologically compulsive; it reflects a sadistic tendency in one's character.

Thus, human freedom grounded in autonomy or self-determination extends in two directions. On the one hand, it is characterized by *resistance* to psychological and cultural determinations, and, on the other, by the deliberate *construction* of an individuality unique and authentic to oneself, or self-actualization. It is evident that self-actualization, as an ultimate end of moral conduct, embraces a total life career. One may say that the prime objective of ethical conduct is to discover a form of personal existence which one must propose to oneself as the intent of one's being and to the realization of which one must *consistently* devote the whole of oneself.

Our two-fold conception of freedom, which is seen to flow from our conception of the ethical agent, gives us a two-fold set of criteria,

---

* *The Fundamental Principles of the Metaphysics of Ethics*, p. 48. Italics in the parentheses are the author's.

which are designed to guide the ethical agent in his choice of appropriate courses of action. These criteria are: (1) resistance and (2) constructivity. In resolving a given moral conflict, the ethical agent must make certain, firstly, that the course of action he chooses involves resistance to dominant pressures from within and without; and secondly, that the chosen action is constructive of the form of personality he seeks to realize, that it is consistent with the self-proposed intent of his being.

Obviously, these criteria require elaboration and more definitive clarification, especially in the light of their application to concrete ethical situations. This will be done after we have elaborated on the dynamic character traits that go into the making of the ethical agent. For the present, this set of criteria is designed to make clear that while an ethical theory derived from the primacy of the ethical agent is necessarily relativistic, it can still be founded on objective grounds.

CHAPTER FOUR

Individuation—the Construction
of Dynamic Character

FREEDOM FROM DOMINATION and freedom for constructive, self-designed, self-reliant, self-determined living are integrally entwined: one is dependent upon the other. Freedom from and freedom for stand to one another in the relation of means and ends or acts and motives. Unless the quest of freedom from outer restraint or inner compulsion is motivated by a powerful urge or desire to achieve an individuality unique to oneself, one cannot be certain whether a person's resistance to dominant pressures is more than mere psychological rebellion.

It is obvious that similar manifestations of resistance to conformity may causally derive from vastly different sources. The wide divergence of causal factors is the result of differences in psychological make-up or cultural environment, or a combination of both. It is important, therefore, that we distinguish between the type of resistance which reflects an individual's inability to adjust effectively to his environment and the type of resistance which reflects a deliberate striving for self-expression.

Psychologists tell us that among the diversity of impulses and drives are the drive for dependence and the drive for autonomy. We have pointed out in the previous chapter that the adult world tends to suppress the drive to autonomy and to exploit the drive to dependence in a more or less calculated design to preserve established traditions. Those who deny or refuse to recognize the fact of "child exploitation" tend to describe it as the natural process of socialization (a subtle form of rationalization). If this process of "socialization" is subtly manipulated, the growing individual will, in all likelihood, integrate himself wholesomely in his social environment. If, however, the pressures become excessively inhibitive, they are likely to produce emotional disturbances and erratic patterns of behavior. So far from integrating the youth in his social environment, these pressures tend to alienate the individual, making him hostile, antagonistic, and rebellious to discipline and molding influences. This type of background gives us, at best, the "rebel without a cause," the "angry young man," and the self-styled expatriot, and, at worst, the deeply neurotic and the criminal. While all these types are caught up in campaigns of resistance, their psychological defiance is not likely to lead to personal independence. On the contrary, having been alienated from one environment, they tend to seek, often more desperately, belongingness in out-groups, where group identification operates through symbols, rituals, and thought patterns as rigid and dominant as those of the in-groups. Psychological defiance which springs from compulsive alienation from one's social environment is *collective* rather than *individualistic* in character. The type of resistance required for unique individuality stems from an entirely different source. It has its inception in a careful nurture of a drive for autonomy, where the growing individual is encouraged to become self-reliant—to resist adaptive pressures, to be curious and explorative, to make free decisions wherever warranted, and to express those aspects of his psychological make-up which lead to differentiation from collective thinking and feeling.

Psychologists are hard put when it comes to identifying those aspects of character which constitute individuality. This is confirmed by C. G. Jung's analysis of the role of psychology as a science:

> . . . to speak of a science of individual psychology is already a contradiction in terms. It is only the collective element in the psychology of an individual that constitutes an object for science; for the individual is by definition a unique reality that cannot be compared with anything else.*

Because psychology, like all other sciences, finds it difficult to treat of the unique and individual in its subject matter, stress has

---

* C. G. Jung, *Two Essays on Analytical Psychology*, transl. by R. F. C. Hull, Meridian Books, N. Y., 1956, p. 295.

been laid upon those aspects which are collective, i.e., the general adjustmental processes in human development. Take, for example, G. W. Allport's definition of personality in which the emphasis on adjustment is clearly evident. For him personality is "the dynamic organization within the individual of those psychophysical systems that determine his unique adjustments to his environment."* While this definition refers to the dynamic, as well as the unique aspects of personality, it characterizes these aspects in terms of their function in the total process of adjustment. The "psychological systems" that determine adjustment are generally described in terms of pervasive psychological categories, such as dispositions, needs, interests, and tendencies. Robert W. White, in his book, *The Abnormal Personality*, gives a concise characterization of "psychophysical systems that determine adjustments."

> When fixed and routine, these systems are often called *habits;* when more generalized and flexible, *dispositions.* If the element of craving or desire is prominent, they are apt to be called *needs,* but if particular objects or channels of expression loom in the foreground it seems more appropriate to speak of *interests.* When the objects of interest happen to be public events or social problems, the words *attitude* or *sentiment* are usually chosen. At this point we want an inclusive single term, so we shall simply call all these things *tendencies.* A person's daily and yearly life can be described as a series of tendencies, and his personality is the more or less organized pattern of these tendencies, his *personal pattern of tendencies.***

It is obvious that with the emphasis upon adjustment, motivation and learning—the basic factors in human development—are inevitably geared to the end of cultivating the kind of individual who is able to play his role in society, effectively and reliably. C. G. Jung makes the point that the process of adjustment is in inverse ratio to the process of individuation. The more we adjust to what society demands of us, to the role it assigns to us, the more we are likely

---

* G. W. Allport, *Personality: A Psychological Interpretation*, New York, Henry Holt and Co., 1937, p. 48.
** Robert W. White, *The Abnormal Personality*, p. 106.

to suppress those character traits which make us uniquely distinct from the collective ideal of a well-functioning social being.

> Society expects, and indeed must expect, every individual to play the part assigned to him as perfectly as possible, so that a man who is a parson must not only carry out his official functions objectively, but must at all times and in all circumstances play the role of parson in a flawless manner. Society demands this as a kind of surety; each must stand at his post, here a cobbler, there a poet. No man is expected to be both. Nor is it advisable to be both, for that would be 'queer.' Such a man would be 'different' from other people, not quite reliable. . . . To present an unequivocal face to the world is a matter of practical importance. . . . Our society is undoubtedly set on such an ideal. Obviously no one could completely submerge his individuality in these expectations; hence the construction of an artificial personality becomes an unavoidable necessity. The demands of propriety and good manners are an added inducement to assume a becoming mask. What goes on behind the mask is then called 'private life.' This painfully familiar division of consciousness into two figures, often preposterously different, is an incisive psychological operation that is bound to have repercussions on the unconscious.*

All this bears out our basic contention that the price we pay for belongingness within society plays havoc, not only with psychic health, but also with human integrity and human freedom. If human freedom is to be preserved, then C. G. Jung's warning against the moral corrosion engendered by integration in a dominant society ought not to go unheeded.

> It is a notorious fact that the morality of society as a whole is in inverse ratio to its size; for the greater the aggregation of individuals, the more the individual factors are blotted out, and with them morality, which rests entirely on the moral sense of the individual and the freedom necessary for this. Hence every man is, in a certain sense, unconsciously a worse man when

---
* C. G. Jung, *Two Essays on Analytical Psychology*, p. 203.

he is in society than when acting alone; for he is carried by society and to that extent relieved of his individual responsibility. Any large company composed of wholly admirable persons has the morality and intelligence of an unwieldy, stupid, and violent animal. The bigger the organization, the more unavoidable is its immorality and blind stupidity. (Senatus bestia, senatores boni viri).*

Thus, it becomes clearly evident that the destiny of freedom today rests solely with our ethical agent, the kind of individual who is able, not only to resist the conforming pressures of his society—to break away from the dominant practices, beliefs, and goals of his cultural environment—but also to make his resistance the dynamic *means* of a creative process of individuation. While it is difficult for psychology to explicate the exact nature of individuality, many psychologists today are engaged in fruitful research into the factors essential to the process of individuation, as well as into the type of background in which these factors are likely to be fostered. To elaborate on this would take our study too far afield. For our purposes a summary account will be adequate. The findings converge on the following factors as constitutive aspects of dynamic personality: (1) explorative, imaginative thinking, (2) empathy, (3) autonomy, (4) creativity, and (5) marginality.

(1) *Explorative, imaginative thinking:* In contrast to synthesizing thinking which integrates what is already known, unifying or harmonizing existent facts in a logical, well-organized, orderly manner, explorative imaginative thinking is essentially originative, enabling us to look at things in a new and different way. It makes for discovery and innovation. In the interpersonal sphere, it is the kind of thinking that enables us to discover new and more satisfying ways to interact with others. Foote and Cottrell, in their book *Identity and Interpersonal Competence,* define this type of thinking as "the actor's capacity to free himself from established routines of perception and action and to redefine situations and act in the new roles called for by the situations." In marked contrast to formal, conventional relationships in which everyone's behavior is culturally determined,

---

* *Ibid,* pp. 162-163.

explorative thinking is characterized by inventiveness in social relationships. It is especially marked by the capacity for critical judgment, the ability to estimate and evaluate the consequences to oneself
of alternate lines of conduct, to adjudicate among values, etc.

(2) *Empathy*: Empathy is taken to be the ability correctly to
interpret the attitudes and intentions of others; to perceive situations
from another's standpoint; to "take the role of the other" in anticipation and prediction of another's behavior.

(3) *Autonomy*: In the characterization of individuality, psychologists take autonomy to be perhaps the most essential element. By
autonomy psychologists mean these aspects: the clarity of the individual's conception of self (identity); the extent to which he
maintains a stable set of self-proposed standards by which he acts;
the degree to which he is self-directed and self-controlled in his actions; his confidence in and reliance upon himself; the degree of
self-respect he maintains; and the capacity for recognizing real threats
to self and of mobilizing realistic defenses when so threatened.

(4) *Creativity*: Psychologists are hard put in defining this factor
in the process of individuation. Broadly speaking, it is characterized
as a demonstrable capacity for innovations in behavior or for reconstruction of any aspect of one's social environment. It involves
the ability to develop fresh perspectives from which to view accepted
routines, to make novel combinations of ideas and objects and infuse
established goals with fresh meaning, inventing means for their realization. In interpersonal relations it is the ability to invent or
improvise new roles or alternative lines of action in problematic
situations. Among other things, it involves curiosity, venturesomeness,
"risk-taking tendencies of the explorer," flexibility of attitude, and
open-mindedness.

(5) *Marginality*: This aspect of individuation is developed by
R. E. Park in his book, *Race and Culture*. He defines marginality
as the ability to stand outside of one's culture, to remain *uninvolved*
with organizational life, and to strike out in new paths of thought
and action. The marginal man is he who is not bound, as others
are, by parochial conventions and mores. Since he is not determined
by his culture's customs and beliefs, he can be more objective in
his judgments. The marginal man has the capacity to innovate fresh
perspectives, not only because he *resists* the dominance of his culture,

but also because his isolation permits him to reflect critically on his culture's pervasive thought patterns.

While these factors overlap, they focus on character traits which, as will be seen, are indispensable conditions for objective valuation. In addition to providing us with guide lines for becoming an ethical agent, psychologists have done considerable research into the type of background which favors the emergence of the ethical agent. In a study, "Some Relationships Between Family Background and Personality,"* J. Carpenter and P. Eisenberg report that in homes in which "freedom" and "individuality" were stressed children grew into "dominant" personalities, whereas "adult-dominated" homes produced, to a large degree, "submissive" adults —shy, dependent, and anxious. P. M. Symonds in his book *Psychology of Parent-Child Relationships,* reports similar findings. He found the children from stricter homes courteous, obedient and neat, but also more shy, timid, withdrawing, docile, and troubled. His study indicates that the more permissive parent brings up children who are more aggressive and more disobedient, but who are also more self-confident, more effective at self-expression, and more independent. A. L. Baldwin in his book on *Socialization and the Parent-Child Relationship* found that highly authoritative homes are likely to have children who are seriously restricted in curiosity, originality, and imagination.

All in all, psychological studies corroborate a direct correlation between permissiveness in the home and the emergence of independence and creativity in the growing individual. However, psychologists also emphasize that while a favorable social climate may be a strong contributing factor to the creation of individuality, it is neither a sufficient, nor even a necessary, condition for it. They point to the life histories of creative personalities in the arts, the sciences, politics, etc., whose backgrounds are so divergent in nature as to make predictions in individual cases utterly unwarranted. However, the autobiographies of such personalities indicate that the basic factor in the emergence of an independent, highly creative personality is a powerful urge for uniqueness, originality, and creativity. Without such a powerful drive, an individual is not likely to overcome the

---

* *Journal of Psychology,* 1938, pp. 115-136.

mighty obstacles wrought by the pressures of a dominant society. C. G. Jung defines this drive to individuality as a "vocation" which an individual must cultivate consciously and deliberately and sustain throughout his life:

> Only the man who is able *consciously* to affirm the power of the vocation confronting him from within becomes a personality.*

In order to discover what is authentically individual in ourselves, we must first acquire a knowledge of our potentialities; we must explore those capacities in our constitutional being which permit us to be at our best, which enable us to achieve excellence in a chosen field of endeavor. We must make sure that the sole motive for choosing one field rather than another be the achievement of competence —the realization of our best potential. Of course, it is fairly obvious that most people make themselves believe that what has come to be their life occupation is a career which they have not only consciously chosen, but for which they are eminently suited. Unless we can convince ourselves that we are ideally fitted for our profession, the outsiders—those who judge us or seek our services—are not likely to have the desired confidence in us. It is a notorious fact that most people tend to rationalize away their inadequacies and inflate those capacities and skills which are requisite and essential to the profession in which they happen to be engaged. If the exploration of our potentialities is to be accurate, we must be ready to test what we have discovered as being authentic to us by objective standards of evaluation. It is fairly obvious that we are not likely to achieve excellence, not to speak of creativity, in any field, so long as our life pursuits are motivated by non-intrinsic ends such as social approbation, recognition, power, or economic security. This is the reason why Jung regards the exploration of one's potentialities as a vocation. Unless we are *sincere* with ourselves, we cannot *do right* by ourselves.

Are there criteria by which we can judge whether or not we are accurate in the evaluation of our capacities and potentialities? We can take our cue from certain psychological insights. There is, for one, spontaneity, and, for another, the sense of self-rewarding grati-

---

* C. G. Jung, *The Integration of the Personality*, London, Routledge & Kegan Paul, Ltd., 1950, p. 295.

fication. Those activities which spring from a spontaneous impulse, to which we seem irresistibly drawn by inclination, are far more likely to reveal to us our capacities than activities to which we come by circumstance or outer direction. It is also true that when we find the things we do to be self-rewarding, we are moving in a direction which aims at self-expression and self-realization, we are operative in an area where our real capacities are being constructively mobilized.

To become an ethical agent or, in other words, to achieve personal freedom, in its dual aspects, the process of individuation—the exploration and cultivation of one's inherent possibilities—must go hand in hand with the process of integration. We must consciously and deliberately organize our differentiated tendencies into a hierarchy of standards and goals so that certain tendencies assume superior status over others, controlling or inhibiting them as the occasion demands. Functioning effectively as an ethical agent—the setting of stable standards and distant goals, the making of and acting upon moral decisions in conflict situations, the reconstructing of existent values within an intellectualized framework of one's own, the battle against dominant pressures—all of this implies a high degree of organization. It implies a wholeness of being, a unitary character structure so ordered that the tendencies and goals which we affirm to be of most importance are given priority over the less important.

Some writers believe that it is unwarranted to assume the existence of separate tendencies, urges, or drives. K. Goldstein, for instance, maintains that "the facts which are taken as foundations for the assumption of different drives are more or less abstractions from the natural behavior of the organism." He, therefore, posits "only one drive, the drive of self-actualization," manifesting itself in different ways under different circumstances. In Goldstein's view, there is no need to introduce a special concept to point to the unity of the organism. The unity is present from the start and should be implicit in everything we say about separate tendencies.*

Goldstein fails to draw characteristic distinctions between the drives of a lower animal and those of a human being. To speak of a

---

* K. Goldstein, *Human Nature and Psychopathology*, Cambridge, Harvard University Press, 1940, pp. 144-145.

single drive of self-actualization may be appropriate in characterizing the behavior of an animal, whose drives are completely blind and unconscious, determined by nature, well-nigh fully developed from the time of birth. However, in respect to a human being, it is important that we take account of certain distinct characteristics which make him unique in the animal kingdom. There is, firstly, the consciousness of one's drives, secondly, the capacity not only to differentiate collective tendencies, but also to integrate them into a dynamic character structure, and thirdly, the capacity to fashion a structured organization of purposes and goals. On the negative side, a human being can, unlike other animals, incur neurotic disorganization and possible breakdown in consequence of maladjustment. Clearly, writers like K. Goldstein reflect the thinking of behavioristically oriented psychologists whose basic weakness is the failure to distinguish significantly between observable behavior patterns and their underlying dynamic character traits.

In the human being, the drive of self-actualization, so far from being a causally determined process in nature, is a dynamic creative enterprise powered by an inspired moral force. C. G. Jung makes this point when he insists that ". . . personality can never develop itself unless the individual chooses his own way consciously and with conscious moral decision. Not only the causal motive, the need, but a conscious moral decision must lend its strength to the process of the development of personality."*

Thus, a dynamic character structure, one in which differentiated tendencies have been integrated into a coherent whole, must be seen as the culmination or end-product of a conscious, deliberate endeavor by the kind of individual who has worked out for himself a carefully designed blueprint of his life. Obviously, men do not acquire dynamic character in the same way in which they acquire peculiar tastes or mannerisms. Self-discipline, self-respect, self-reliance, independence of judgment and conviction, empathy, inventiveness, open-mindedness, insight into and actualization of one's unique capacities—all these dynamic traits which we prize as attributes of ethical character cannot be seen as mere causal by-products of man's adjustmental reactions to his environment. Rather than mere psychological entities, these dis-

---

* *The Integration of the Personality*, p. 289.

tinctive character traits must be taken to be moral *values* or *virtues* which a man must choose and cultivate as he must all other values. Such traits can only be understood in the context of a total dynamic organization from which single character traits must be seen to flow.

Thus, our inquiry into the question, "How does an individual become an ethical agent?" has led us into a basic tradition in moral philosophy, one which is generally identified as teleological "perfectionism" or humanism. Such systems conceive of man's chief good as consisting in the fulfilling or maturing or perfecting of potentialities that lie within him. In such systems the ultimate end of man is taken to be self-realization. While ethical thinkers are generally agreed that this tradition embodies the noblest aims of man, they are critical of it because it treats of such concepts as the "self" or "realization" in terms too vague and generalized. It is held that self-realization as a principle of morality lacks sufficient concreteness to be meaningful as a guide in the resolution of specific, ordinary moral issues. In analyzing what constitutes human potentialities and unique abilities and how these are to be engendered, it has been our objective to explicate the concept of self-realization by a thorough reliance on recent psychological findings. We have attempted to show that self-realization, in concrete terms, constitutes the construction of a rounded, well-organized character structure along the lines of differentiation as well as integration. We have not only pointed out obstacles which a person must overcome to develop a dynamic character structure, but also the kind of tendencies he must cultivate to achieve self-realization. We have indicated that unless the construction of dynamic character is motivated by a powerful moral force, one cannot hope to bring it to fruition.

It becomes evident that the creation of dynamic character requires the conception of self as an "end in itself." (We shall elaborate on this in Chapters 6 and 7.) Again, this is in keeping with Kant's principle that "humanity and every rational nature is an *end in itself*."* We apply this principle not only to the attitudes and actions of an individual in his treatment of others, but also to man's relation to himself. We can thus interpret the moral force required for the creation of dynamic character in terms of the demand that in his

---

* *The Fundamental Principles of the Metaphysics of Ethics*, p. 48.

personality development a person must treat himself as an end rather than as a tool to the furtherance of ambitions and drives which prove, in the long run, to be actual hindrances to self-realization.

In explicating the concept of self-realization, we have constantly kept in mind our objective to establish adequate foundations for the attainment of freedom—freedom *from* compulsive restraints and freedom *for* constructive, self-designed living. Freedom *from* involves the obstacles to self-realization, and freedom *for* involves the means by which it is attained. A person can be said to be free or self-determined if, and only if, on the one hand, he is effectively resisting both psychological and cultural determinations, and, on the other hand, his actions flow from a total dynamic character structure. In the light of this, the concept of a rational moral agent takes on concrete meaningfulness. One can say that a rational ethical agent is he who aims at self-realization, who conceives of himself as an end in itself, whose total pattern of behavior is grounded in dynamic character. A person may speak a moral language, avow moral principles, and believe his actions to be free, but so long as he fails to comply with our characterization of a rational agent, he cannot be said to think or act in a genuine moral sense. This we shall attempt to demonstrate in our next chapter, in which we shall seek to establish the foundations of objective valuation.

CHAPTER FIVE

Constructive Dynamic Reason

A BASIC IMPLICATION of the primacy of the ethical agent is the demand for a contextual analysis of moral reasoning as it bears upon moral character. To do justice to the factors and distinctions characteristic of the nature of moral reasoning, it is essential to recognize its functional dependence on and organic interrelation with moral character.

The thesis that moral character is an indispensable prerequisite for moral reasoning has a respectable tradition in ethics. Perhaps none has supported it more firmly than Aristotle, the dean of ethical thinkers. According to Aristotle, moral reasoning consists essentially of two basic factors: (1) deliberation over means, and (2) projection of ends. He holds that a person who deliberates well over the means for the attainment of certain ends is not necessarily one who can be said to be morally wise, or to act in a genuine moral sense. He corroborates this thesis by a careful distinction between "cleverness" and "practical wisdom."* Cleverness is excellence in deliberation, and while it involves reasoning, it attests only to the accuracy or "correctness of thinking" and not to the adequacy of *moral* reasoning. Practical wisdom, on the other hand, while it includes cleverness, requires, in addition, the possession of moral virtues. For Aristotle, virtues are not just conceptual entities, but rather organic aspects of a man's total personality structure. So he defines virtues as "active states of character."** Thus, in addition to deliberating effectively in the choice of appropriate means, we require virtuous character in

---

* Aristotle, "Ethica Nicomachea" (henceforth E. N.), translated by W. D. Ross, *The Basic Works of Aristotle,* ed. by Richard McKeon, Random House, New York, 1141a 33-1141b. 5. See also 1144a 24-1145a 6.
** E. N. 1105a 34.

order to project what can be said to be proper moral ends. While deliberation determines the correctness of the choice of means, virtuous character determines the adequacy of the projection of ends. "Therefore," Aristotle concludes, "it is evident that it is impossible to be practically wise without being good."*

The basic thesis, then, of Aristotelian ethics, is the insistence that moral character is prior to moral reasoning. We do not become ethical by learning about ethics, by acquiring a knowledge of ethical rules and maxims, or, of the logical schema of moral reasoning. Rather, we become ethical by living ethically, by a sustained, life-long nurture and practice of ethical patterns of conduct. A person must first become an ethical human being, in experience, before he can be said to reason morally or to act in a genuine moral sense. Whether an action is good or bad, right or wrong, is dependent entirely upon the kind of character structure from which the action flows. This we have recognized as a basic implication of the primacy of the ethical agent. It is fully corroborated by Aristotelian thought:

> Actions, then, are called just and temperate when they are such as the just or the temperate man would do; but it is not the man who does these that is just and temperate, but the man who also does them *as* just and temperate men do them. It is well said, then, that it is by doing just acts that the just man is produced, and by doing temperate acts the temperate man; without doing these no one would have even a prospect of becoming good.**

Implicit in all this is our principle of the primacy of the ethical agent. This principle basically implies that the requisite conditions on the basis of which adequate moral judgments are possible reside in the ethical agent, in the kind of man who can properly be said to be a truly ethical human being. This, too, is corroborated by Aristotle. In distinguishing between the arts and virtues, Aristotle is emphatic in his insistence that while valuation in the arts is dependent on the substance of the artistic products alone, in the case of

---

* E. N. 1144a 36-37.
** E. N. 1105b 5-12.

the virtues, the criteria of valuation reside in the man rather than in his performances.

> . . . The case of the arts and that of the virtues are not similar; for the products of the arts have their goodness in themselves, so that it is enough that they should have a certain character, but if the acts that are in accordance with the virtues have themselves a certain character it does not follow that they are done justly or temperately. The agent must be in a certain condition when he does them; in the first place he must have knowledge, secondly he must choose the acts, and choose them for their own sakes, and thirdly, his action must proceed from a firm and unchangeable character.*

According to Aristotle, then, the efficacy of moral reasoning as well as the appropriateness of moral action, hinges upon the firmness and stability of character. While Aristotle is not explicit in what he means by a "firm and unchangeable character," he does, in a sense, corroborate our thesis that the construction of *dynamic* character is an indispensable prerequisite for reasoning or acting morally. Aristotle bears out our contention that unaided by certain dynamic character traits, the power of reason cannot be relied on as an effective instrument in the mastery of moral conduct.

It is evident, then, that a theory of moral reasoning, if it is to be adequate, must take account of personality structure as a coherent whole, in which certain definitive reasoning processes and certain definitive traits and tendencies are made jointly operative in the practical sphere of human conduct. To divorce the analysis of the role and function of moral reasoning from an elucidation of moral character is to lose sight, not only of its limitations, but also of certain essential features in its operations.

The current despair in the rationality of ethics is a consequence of the disillusionment with a naive rationalism which entrusted the guidance and control of human conduct to the power of reason alone. We need not succumb to this despair once we acknowledge the limitations of moral reasoning in the mastery of moral conduct. We

---

* E. N. 1105a 28-35.

must begin to realize that moral reasoning can be an effective instrument of moral conduct *only* if it is grounded in a dynamic character structure. (We have set forth in the previous chapter the nature of the character structure and the ways by which it is brought into being.) Moral reasoning must be seen as a kind of potency which requires, to become operative, a determinable set of traits and tendencies that makes for autonomy and self-reliance.

In focussing on the primacy of the ethical agent, it has become evident that the supreme end of the moral life is self-actualization, or the fully actualized ethical personality. Viewed from this perspective, the ultimate objective of moral reasoning involves two basic aspects: (1) the vision of oneself as a fully developed life-form of being, and (2) the organic process of self-actualization by which this self-proposed vision of life-form is brought into being. To the extent that actualization of the vision of one's life-form is achieved in existence, an individual can be said to live by the dictates of moral reasoning. Or, in other words: the extent of self-actualization measures the degree to which the potency of moral reasoning is made operative in moral conduct.

It is, therefore, proper to say that the process of self-actualization —the cultivation of character structure grounded in the dual aspects of freedom—is the essential matrix of ethical existence, the peculiar province of the life of Moral Reason. In it dynamic character traits are developed, ethical habits are established, crucial moral conflicts are encountered and possibly resolved, moral reasoning is made constructively operative.

Now we are in a position to elaborate on our criteria for objective valuation by the ethical agent, namely, resistance and constructivity. We shall see that the criterion of resistance involves the projection of ends, and the criterion of constructivity the determination of the proper means. It is clear that moral reasoning comes into play in the resolution of moral conflicts. To understand the diverse operations of moral reasoning, it is essential that we distinguish between two basic types of moral conflicts: (1) moral conflicts in relation to oneself, and (2) moral conflicts in relation to others. Each type of conflict requires its own distinct pattern of reasoning. It is only in the former that the operation of moral reasoning consists in the deliberation over the appropriate means for the attainment of self-proposed ends. In the latter, the pattern of moral reasoning contains the following facets: arbitration between conflicting demands, clarification of opposing interpretations of the facts, and often conciliation between underlying clashing emotive attitudes.*

The proper domain for the application of our two criteria, resistance and constructivity, is the arena of those moral conflicts in which the ethical agent stands in relation to himself only, where he encounters moral problems that concern his own needs and aspirations. Constructivity means that the agent's choice of means—means being diverse courses of action—must be conducive to his deliberate endeavor at self-actualization. When we say that an act is *constructive of the ethical agent,* we mean, then, that in his choice between alternative courses of action he has given priority to the one that is most likely to advance self-proposed, long-range ends.

The criterion of resistance, on the other hand, guides the agent in the selection of ends, those which are relevant, instrumental to the ultimate goal of self-actualization. In order to make certain that his values are freely chosen, that they are, indeed, instrumental to self-realization, he must first determine whether or not he is effectively resisting those cultural and psychological determinations which cause most individuals to accept ideals and values that are dominant in their society.

In order to apply effectively our criteria for objective valuation, the ethical agent must have, in addition to dynamic character, a distinct body of knowledge (we have seen that among the three conditions for adequate moral action Aristotle cites "knowledge"). What type of knowledge must a person have to qualify as a moral agent, i.e., an autonomous, self-reliant personality? Essentially the knowledge he requires must be such as to enable him, on the one hand, to resist inner compulsive urges and outer dominant pressures, and, on the other, to realize his ultimate life-form—the vision of himself as a fully developed being in whom unique capacities have been brought to complete fruition. Thus, to operate effectively as an

---

* In regard to conciliation between clashing attitudes, C. L. Stevenson's distinction between disagreement in belief and disagreement in attitude is highly enlightening. See his article on "The Nature of Ethical Disagreement" in *Readings in Philosophical Analysis,* ed. by H. Feigl and W. Sellers, Appleton Century-Crofts, Inc., New York, 1949.

ethical agent, a person must acquire, as has been already stated, a two-fold body of knowledge: (1) self-knowledge and (2) knowledge of one's culture's pervasive traits and purposes.

Self-knowledge involves not only a clear conception of the kind of individual one is, but also of the kind of personality one ultimately seeks to become. It is evident that without a profound comprehension of our real interests and unique abilities we cannot plan our future, we cannot construct a proper "life-form" in which what we are authentically—the truth of our being—can be fully actualized. Without this dual knowledge an ethical agent cannot make adequate value judgments in the resolution of his moral conflicts.. He cannot know *what* means are appropriate or *what* ends are instrumental to his striving for self-actualization. This is borne out by Aristotle in his insistence that "we deliberate about things that are in our power and can be done."* In judging what we ought to do under given circumstances, we must know what, in fact, we can do, what lies within our power to realize.

There is in vogue in current academic circles the slogan, "Ought implies can."** It is clear from what we have said that if there be such an implication, it is far from a logical one. It is a notorious fact that most people have exaggerated opinions of their real capacities and tend to rationalize away their limitations. If "ought" is to imply "can," our dual body of knowledge must be pre-supposed. Only a person who acquires it is a person of whose value judgments one might say that "ought" does, indeed, imply "can." This is a determination, however, which only the agent himself can make in respect to his own value judgments—the choice of means appropriate for the utilization of his capacities and the projection of ends relevant to self-actualization.

All this is in accord with our basic thesis of ethical relativism, which we have seen to flow from the principle of the primacy of the ethical agent. As has been previously pointed out, ethical relativism must not be confused with what goes in present academic circles as subjectivism. We take our stand with objectivism, but in a limited sense only. Valuation can be objective if, and only if, it is

---

* E. N.
** See, for example, R. M. Hare's discussion on " 'Ought' and 'Can' " in his book, *Freedom and Reason*, pp. 51-56.

made by an ethical agent in the resolution of moral conflicts which relate only to himself, or, in other words, which he encounters in the process of self-actualization. We have stated the conditions as well as the criteria on the basis of which objective valuation, as relevant to the ethical agent, is possible. One of the conditions is, as we have seen, self-knowledge in a dual sense, knowledge of the self as it is and of the self as we intend it to be. In the resolution of moral conflicts relevant to ourselves only, we operate with our total personality, and only insofar as we have a sound understanding of it can we be said to have control over our actions. One can say, therefore, that character as realized is the instrumentality for the construction of character yet to be realized.

In deliberating over the means for the projection of ends, adequacy of valuation consists essentially in the determination of the kind of course of action which is best suited for the expression of our real capacities. It is important, therefore, that we draw clear distinctions between the means and the ends in valuation. We cannot be adequate in the choice of means unless we have first a clear conception of the self that we are, and we cannot be adequate in the projection of ends unless we have first a clear vision of the self that we intend to be. Here, again, we find support in Aristotle's contention that what we deliberate about are the means and not the ends.

> We deliberate not about the ends but about the means. . . The subject of investigation is sometimes the instruments, sometimes the use of them; and similarly in other cases— sometimes the means, sometimes the mode of using it, or the means of bringing it about. It seems then, as has been said, that man is a moving principle of actions; now deliberation is about the things to be done by the agent himself, and actions are for the things other than themselves. For the end cannot be the subject of deliberation, but only the means; . . .*

Aristotle's thesis that in deliberation "the subject of investigation is sometimes the instruments, sometimes the use of them," can be

---

* E. N. 1112b 13-35.

reconstructed for our purposes as follows: We deliberate about the instrumentality of moral action when we explore and get knowledge about our total personality, our true capacities, as well as our limitations. If this be granted, we can take issue with Dewey's conception of the means-ends relationship.

John Dewey's theory of moral reasoning can be seen as an elaboration of Aristotle's position, especially in its emphasis on the relationship between means and ends as the empirical basis for the validity of ethical norms. Valuation, according to him, takes place

> only when there is something the matter; when there is some trouble to be done away with, some need, lack, or privation to be made good, some conflict of tendencies to be resolved by means of changing existing conditions. This fact, in turn, proves that there is present an intellectual factor—a factor of inquiry—whenever there is valuation, for the end-in-view is formed and projected as that which, if acted upon, will supply the existing need or lack and resolve the existing conflict.*

While Dewey relies on Aristotle in his insistence that moral reasoning involves deliberation over means for the attainment of certain ends, his characterization of the means-ends relation is a departure from Aristotle. For Dewey, the latter's insistence "that we deliberate not about ends but about means" is an unwarranted cleavage.

> The end is merely a series of acts viewed at a remote stage; and a means is merely the series viewed at an earlier one. The distinction of means and ends arises in surveying the *course* of a proposed *line* of action, a connected series in time. The 'end' is the last act thought of; the means are the acts to be performed prior to it in time. . . Means and ends are two names for the same reality. The terms denote not a division in reality but a distinction in judgment.**

---

* John Dewey, "The Theory of Valuation," in *International Encyclopedia of Unified Science* (Chicago: The University of Chicago Press, 1939) XI, No. 4, p. 34.

** John Dewey, *Human Nature and Conduct,* The Modern Library, Random House, New York, 1930, pp. 34f.

John Dewey argues that it is unwarranted to separate means from ends in valuation because "we do not know what we are really after until a course of action is mentally worked out."* This is clearly fallacious since it is obvious, as we have shown, that we cannot begin to deliberate over means unless we have first a clear conception of the ends for the realization of which the means are instrumental. Clearly Dewey fails to take account of our principle of the primacy of the ethical agent. The inadequacy of his conception of means and ends relations is attributable to the type of analysis in which the explication of moral concepts and theories is divorced from the context of moral character. We take our stand with Aristotle rather than with Dewey, holding, as the former, that "we deliberate not about ends, but about means."

We have seen that one of the basic aspects of a dynamic character structure—the prerequisite for objective valuation—is the projection of long-range ends to which all other goals must be subordinated. We have also seen that the appropriate long-range ends involve the agent's conception of himself as a life-form to the realization of which he must persistently devote the whole of himself. It becomes clear, then, that what we deliberate about are the means or instrumentalities by which such long-range ends are actualized. Take, for example, a typical moral conflict in the life of a politician. Shall he yield to powerful pressure groups in his constituency or shall he vote his conscience and cast his ballot with what he regards to be in the best interests of the state or the country as a whole, thereby risking his chances for re-election? It is quite obvious that unless a politician is intent on becoming a statesman in the true sense, unless he is so motivated, he is not likely to forego selfish political expediency for the sake of what is demonstrably the bolder course of action.

Dewey's contention that "we do not know what we are really after until a course of action is mentally worked out" may be true of the kind of person who lacks a knowledge of what he wants to do with his life. But such a person cannot be regarded as an ethical agent in the sense in which we have characterized him. He cannot be said to be the kind of person who is capable of objective valuation

* *Ibid*, p. 36.

in the resolution of his moral conflicts. A person who lacks ultimate goals of life is most likely to be a victim of psychological compulsions from within or dominant pressures from without. The ends of moral conduct cannot be worked out in the process of deliberation over the means. To be freely chosen, they must reflect resistance to values to which most people adhere in their adjustmental efforts in a dominant society. This is why we insist that it is self-knowledge in the dual sense—knowledge of the self as it is and of the self as it is intended to be—which provides the basis for the projection of ends and the selection of the appropriate means to realize initially self-proposed ends. Without self-knowledge, adequate application of our criteria of resistance and constructivity is impossible.

In addition to self-knowledge the ethical agent must have, for objective valuation (as has been previously pointed out), a substantive knowledge of his culture's prevalent mores, traditions, and beliefs. In this complex technological age, he must have a keen awareness of the relativity of ethico-social norms and standards, of the entrenchment of established beliefs, of the massed obstacles to change inherent in social structure, and of the pervasive conformity which has overcome the overwhelming majority in our society today. The extent to which this type of sophistication characterizes a person's choice of values measures the degree to which objectivity is reflected in his valuation.

All this reinforces our basic thesis that objective valuation or adequate moral reasoning is dependent upon specifiable conditions inherent in the ethical agent. It equally underscores the demand for a contextual analysis of moral values as it bears upon moral character. Recent efforts to explicate the character of moral reasoning in terms of analogies from science have proven, by and large, to be unenlightening. The basic reason for this is the failure to recognize the functional dependence upon and the organic interrelation of moral reasoning with moral character.

We must begin to realize that moral reasoning in practical affairs must be clearly distinguished from theoretical reasoning in the sphere of knowledge. Moral reasoning and theoretical reasoning are incommensurate operations. They differ not only in methodology—the logical character of their apparatus—but also in the objectives to which their respective methodologies are seen to be instrumental. The methods of theoretical reasoning are observation, experimentation, and verification. Theoretical reasoning is hypothetico-deductive in character. It involves the construction of hypotheses for the explanation of apparent regularities in observable data, and the testing of their validity in terms of the fruitfulness of their consequences. The objective of theoretical reasoning is the unification of knowledge into a systematized body of theories and laws. Moral reasoning, on the other hand, consists essentially, as we have seen, in the deliberation over means—actions flowing from a certain type of character structure—for the attainment of ends which are integrally tied up with the total process of self-actualization.

To make clear the incommensurability of reasoning in science and reasoning in practical conduct, it is essential that we draw the following distinction: theoretical reasoning in the sphere of knowledge is instrumental to the control and mastery of physical nature; moral reasoning in the sphere of conduct is instrumental to the control and mastery of human nature. We can express this distinction in another way: reasoning in science aims at the construction of observable data into systematic knowledge; reasoning in the sphere of conduct aims at the construction of character into a coherent whole—a structured organization of dynamic character traits, a hierarchical system of purposes and ends.

To fully appreciate the constructive and dynamic character of reason in human conduct, it is of primary importance that we distinguish between adequate moral reasoning and its pseudo-counterpart, rationalization. This, in turn, will shed light on what is taken to be the crisis of our times—the dominance of irrationality. The differences between moral reasoning and rationalization can be seen as the clear implications of the role and function of reason in the resolution of those moral conflicts that involve the ethical agent only. We can differentiate as follows:

(1) Moral reasoning is *self-revelatory, self-expressive;* rationalization is *self-deceptive, self-inhibitive.* We have shown that if moral reasoning is to be adequate, it must, in the deliberation over appropriate means, seize upon that course of action which is most likely to be constructive of the self as a life-form, to the realization of which a person must devote his best efforts and capacities. It is evident that in so doing we are made to draw on our deepest resources, those

83

which constitute our genuine potential for creative self-expression. Thus, in the process of adequate moral reasoning, a person is made to *reveal* to himself that which is authentically unique to him as a person, those aspects of his personality which make for creativity, for genuine productive achievements. To illustrate the revelatory character of adequate moral reasoning, take, for example, the case of a young professional academician who is confronted with this moral choice: shall he write articles for journals to secure tenure in conformity with the insidious trend to "publish or perish"; or shall he risk his job security and devote his efforts to long-range creative endeavors, spending years in research and writing before he can hope to see his work in print? Clearly, the proper moral decision is to choose the latter course despite the risks to job security. However, it is a determination which few are willing to make, not only because it is the more difficult course of action, but because it sets aside immediate benefits for promises that not only lie in the distant future, but the realization of which is highly uncertain. Few, indeed, are ready to test their real capacities, to reveal to themselves their limitations as well as their creative possibilities. The fact is that most people choose the more expedient course dictated by the quests for security, recognition, or power. And in the course of it, they cover up by allegedly rational explanations—so-called good reasons—their inability to pursue long-range goals of creative achievement. The result is self-deception and the inhibition of our real abilities and talents. In the light of this, current sociological findings which attest to the suppression of creativity in the upper ranks of management in industry become fully understandable. As has been pointed out, today's pressures to conformity cause even the dynamic among the executive personnel to cover up by rationalization the surrender of the control over their own destiny, rather than to resist these pressures and to keep faith with autonomy and creative productivity.

(2) Moral reasoning is *objective;* rationalization is *subjective.* Moral reasoning, if it is adequate, furnishes for the justification of the choice of a given course of action, *warranted* reasons which are grounded, as we have seen, in a two-fold body of knowledge—knowledge of self in a dual sense and knowledge of one's culture. In addition, valuation here is guided by appropriate criteria, namely, resistance and constructivity. Rationalization, on the other hand, has

no such foundations. It furnishes for the justification of the choice of a given course of action *pseudo* reasons, or allegedly rational explanations for compliance with what are, in truth, drives or anxieties whose compulsive nature we have failed to recognize.

(3) The crucial difference between reasoning and rationalization, the one which is causally responsible for (1) and (2), is the difference in character structure. Moral reasoning is grounded, as we have seen, in dynamic, highly individualized character; rationalization flows from the type of character structure which is lacking in differentiation and/or integration. Psychologists have made it clear that persons who fail to integrate interests and tendencies into an ordered personality structure reflect in their conduct erratic, unpredictable patterns of behavior. People lacking in integrated character cannot be rational in conduct. They are fertile ground for the sprouting of irrationality. On the other hand, people whose personality structure is integrated, but lacking in differentiation, reflect a characterology that is described by psychologists as collective rather than individual. Collective characterology is the result, in large measure, of the process of socialization, in which the individual is seen to accommodate himself, in outlook and conduct, to the dominant traits and purposes of his culture. It is the type of character which David Riesman has so effectively described in terms of other-directedness. We have seen that the other-directed individual is the most likely victim of cultural determinations. For this type of individual, rationalization is the instrumentality by which he covers up what is to him, in truth, the real, though unacknowledged, objective of living, an objective which can be colloquially expressed by the slogan, "to keep up with the Joneses." These people live by the values of others, those whom they seek to emulate, rather than by values of their own choosing. If we are to believe current sociological findings, it seems that the overwhelming majority of people in our culture fall into the category of collective characterology. Be that as it may, the conditions and criteria for objective valuation, as laid down in our analysis, highly limit the rank of individuals who are able to apply them in the resolution of their moral problems.

Rationality in conduct, then, can be seen, as the ordering of one's activities in accordance with self-proposed goals of life, in which one's value judgments in the choice of alternative courses of action are grounded in a clear conception of what we are and of what we ultimately intend to become. Rationality in ethics is possible only if it is founded on a determinable character structure in which both integration and differentiation are clearly manifest.

Thus, it has become evident that an explication of moral discourse is unintelligible unless it is directly connected with an elucidation of moral character. So long as we persist in discussing value terms and value judgments outside of the context of character, we cannot hope to escape the confusion which is, in large measure, the result of ethics' insulation within the narrow bounds of the logic of moral language. In the light of our discussion, it can be shown that much of the heated debate between objectivists and subjectivists appears to be artificial and forced. The weakness of both parties lies in the failure to recognize the implications of the primacy of the ethical agent and the inseparable connection between value judgments and the type of man who is seen to make them. As can be expected, both parties are in part right and in part wrong. The subjectivists are right in denying that value terms, such as "good" or "right," stand for special properties, and explaining them, instead, in terms of the agent's basic reactions to objects or actions. However, while they are right in relating value judgments to the agent's interests and attitudes, they are not justified in their reduction of all attitudes and interests to temperamental or emotional preferences. Clearly this reductionist fallacy of subjectivism is attributable to the failure of drawing careful distinctions between constructive, dynamic character traits and those which are determinable purely in terms of tempera- ment and background. Although it cannot be denied that the large majority of people are, indeed, subjective in their valuation, it is improper to infer that *all* value judgments are necessarily subjective in character. This is the kind of generalization that is reflective not only of dogmatism, but also of psychological predilections and/or philosophical preconceptions which, more often than not, underlie a thinker's basic position. The objectivists, on the other hand, are right in their insistence that the characterization of an object or an action as "good" or "right" can be objective. They are wrong, however, in their insistence that the objectivity of values is to be located in either empirical or non-empirical properties or aspects of the thing judged to be "good" or "right." We have seen that the requisite conditions for objective valuation reside in the agent, and that without a clear conception of the agent's character it is impossible to determine whether or not his actions have a genuine moral quality. We have also shown that the determination of something as "good" or "right" is intelligible only in the context of value judgments which involve the agent's *choice* of alternative actions in the resolution of those moral conflicts in which the agent is seen to stand in relation to himself only. It seems apparent, then, that moral discourse is unintelligible if it is divorced from the agent who speaks it, uses it either as a vehicle of communication in relation to others or in the determination of what is proper for him to do under certain circumstances. The logical meaning of words in moral discourse is inseparable from the character structure of the speaker—his basic tendencies and his total set of motives, values, and goals.

Again it can be shown that once we center valuation in the context of character, the controversy between determinism and freedom of will is seen in a new light. The determinists are right in their insistence that a man's actions are determined by his character, his underlying dispositions, tendencies, and attitudes. They are wrong, however, in their conclusion that determinism, in terms of character, precludes the freedom of choice between alternate courses of action. They fail to distinguish between the type of determinism which reflects a collective characterology, molded by an individual's accommodation to his culture's dominant beliefs and patterns of behavior, and the type of determinism which is reflective of a dynamic, highly individualized character structure which, as has been shown, is the culmination of a deliberate, conscious process of self-actualization. Surely dynamic character structure is determined, but it is determined by the individual himself, one who has a clear conception of the "self" as it is and of the "self" which he seeks to realize. This type of determinism must be taken to be self-determination. It must be clearly distinguished from the kind of determinism in which the "self" can be seen in terms of a mechanistically operating organism of conditioned reflexes. The proponents of the freedom of will philosophy are right in their insistence that the reduction of determinism to mechanism robs man of his moral dignity. The weakness of their position, however, lies in their attempt to safeguard the dignity of man by a dubious reliance on what they regard as unique aspects of the human personality, such as "conscience," the power of Reason, etc. They fail to realize that human beings can be, indeed, determined, like all other animals, by constitution and/or environment. The uniqueness of man, so far from being a natural endowment, must be seen as an achievement which is as rare as it is difficult to realize. So G. E. Moore's insistence on the unique and non-natural aspects of moral values is fully justified. However, in the light of our discussion, these unique, non-natural aspects of moral values must not be taken as descriptive of certain properties in objects or ideas, but rather as definitive aspects of character structure. Rather than non-natural properties, it is dynamic character which is unique and irreducible to exclusively empirical terms.

CHAPTER SIX

Commitment

IN CURRENT ETHICAL debate there is the distinction between making a moral decision and committing oneself to acting on it. This distinction is made to account for the fact, borne out by experience, that a person who *knows* what he ought to do is not necessarily a person who can be counted on to do it. While "ought" may imply "can," it does not imply "will be done."

Moral backsliding—failure to keep one's word, change of heart, etc.—is so prevalent in actual interpersonal relationships that unless one is constantly on guard against it, one is likely to become disillusioned with human nature. However, the fact is that the "trusting soul" is a rapidly vanishing phenomenon in our culture. The colloquialism, "Never give a sucker an even break," reflects a callous contempt for one who accepts a promise at face value, who readily believes that what ought to be done and can be done, indeed will be done. Current prophets of doom regard this as symptomatic of a general loss of faith in man, of a pervasive moral apathy which has swept our generation. Is this wholesale condemnation of our generation justifiable? We cannot accept such a sweeping indictment of an age. (Historic records bear out that each generation in the past has been so indicted.)

Today's prevalence of distrust and suspicion of other people's motives reflects not so much man's loss of faith in man as it reflects man's deeper understanding of man. Our generation has not become more depraved in nature, but rather more sophisticated about human nature. As has been previously pointed out, we have, in recent decades, experienced a diffusion of insight into the compulsive aspects of man's behavior patterns. We have learned a good deal about those psychological mechanisms that are causally responsible for what have been decried in the past as manifestations of man's moral weakness. Defense mechanisms, projection mechanisms, inferiority or superiority complexes, phobias, symptom syndromes of neuroses, etc., all these phenomena of social disorganization have come to be common knowledge of the educated layman today. We are not a generation fallen from grace, but rather one which has emerged from the paradise of naiveté and ignorance of the complexities of our psychological dynamism.

Only the untutored in Human Nature are so naive as to believe that the knowledge of moral rules and principles is sufficient for appropriate moral conduct. Men are untrustworthy and unreliable, not because they are ignorant about what is morally required of them, but rather because they are unable, for diverse psychological reasons, to translate into action the "ought" which they mouth in theory. This accounts for the current emphasis on commitment as the necessary link between making a moral judgment and carrying it through in action. However, the assumption of commitment is far from adequate as a basis of moral action so long as we fail to recognize that commitment *per se* is not necessarily moral in character. Unless we analyze the meaning of commitment in the context of character, we shall not be able to differentiate between the type of commitment which can be said to have moral quality and the type of commitment which lacks it.

We have learned, through bitter experience, that commitment can be as damnable as it can be praiseworthy. It can make as easily for blind fanaticism as it can for moral trustworthiness in interpersonal relations. Clearly, the determination of commitment as being moral is dependent upon the nature of its genesis rather than the quality of its being. The loyalty of a Nazi, the heroism of a Japanese suicide pilot, the dedication of a religious fanatic, reflect a commitment no less powerful than the devotion of a scientist in his quest for truth. The essential difference between the former types of commitment and the latter is that while the former reflect domination from without—submission to outer authority—the latter reflects direction from within—adherence to self-proposed ends. The former is the result of indoctrination of one kind or another; the latter is the product of a deliberate cultivation by the individual himself. One can say, then, that commitment is moral in character if, and only if, it is *freely undertaken*—self-inspired, self-determined.

Clearly, commitment is not spontaneous in origin; it is not something which one can decide on instantaneously. Rather it reflects a constancy of being, a set of attributes or complex of qualities, such as steadfastness, dependability, faithfulness, truthfulness, trustworthiness. However, a person may be steadfast, dependable, faithful, truthful, trustworthy, a person may have all these qualities and still be lacking in one essential aspect, the one which would give commitment a moral quality. It is clear that the prerequisite condition for a value to be described as having moral quality is freedom. In viewing freedom from the perspective of the moral agent, we have recognized it to be an attainment—the end of the deliberate, persistent endeavor at self-actualization.

Now we are able to elucidate the significance of commitment in its bearing upon moral conduct. Against the background of our entire discussion, commitment is seen to connote the sustained moral determination which an individual must have to fashion a dynamic character structure unique to himself, which is, so far as it is realized, the means, and so far as it is yet to be realized, the end, of self-actualization. It is this type of commitment which makes the "ought" translatable into action. We can express this as follows: moral judgments are action-guiding if, and only if, they are grounded in action-determining commitment. A person may make a moral judgment and even decide to act on it, but for sundry reasons have a change of heart. The weight of the reasons alone is not sufficient for the determination of moral action. *The decisive factor in moral conduct is moral commitment.*

If moral reasoning is to be the basis for the determination of the appropriate course of action, it requires, in addition to the criteria and conditions set forth in the previous chapter, the force of commitment. In the context of moral character, then, commitment is that aspect of personality which makes a man *conform* in practice to the truths and principles which he avows as the guides of his life. Of course the ultimate truth is the truth of "self"—the vision of the life-form to the realization of which one must devote the major efforts of one's life. Commitment, then, in the deepest sense, is the determination to be true to oneself, the self one is and the self which one intends to realize. The extent to which a person achieves self-realization—the actualization of what is authentically unique to him as a person—measures the degree to which the force of commitment is constructively operative in his conduct.

Commitment to the truth of self which one seeks to realize, or in other words, commitment to the vision of one's life-form, must not be taken as an affirmation of some pre-established essence of being in the traditional sense. So far from constituting a pre-established or even pre-conceived essence, the truth of "self," as defined above, is provisional and tentative, analogous to the "truths" in science which require constant modification in the light of new discoveries. Just as the discovery of a scientific truth is the outcome of an experimental, self-corrective process of exploration, so too, is the discovery of the "truth of self." It consists, as we have already indicated, in the exploration of one's potentialities and the testing of their authenticity in terms of concrete competent productive achievements.

Commitment to the truth of self, then, is the moral determination, firstly, to break away from established patterns of thought and behavior, secondly, to reconstruct the ethico-social values in one's culture by infusing them with fresh, novel meanings, and thirdly, to construct a life-form unique to oneself in which one's genuine or authentic capacities and talents are not only given full expression, but also structured into a coherent whole. All this comprises an evolving process, a persistent, explorative enterprise in which the laboratory of experimentation is seen to be the arena of one's total life career.

Once we recognize the moral nature of commitment, it is no longer feasible to designate as commitments those agreements made in so-called inter-personal relations. What are generally said to be "inter-personal relations" must be taken to be predominantly inter-social or inter-collective relations which are describable empirically in terms of the ethico-social values dominant in a given culture. While it is true, as Dewey maintains, that the individual is a "process in the making," it is important to reiterate that as a product of the process of socialization, man is but an individual replica of collective thinking and feeling, rather than an individual in his own right. Anthropology attests to the fact that the majority of men and women in a dominant society are related to one another in terms of the collective behavior patterns characteristic of their culture. In this inter-collective sphere of human relations, so-called commitment to one's avowed intent is more often than not a necessity for the maintenance of basic social needs and interests. We cannot go on for long, breaking promises or defrauding on agreements with impunity. The building and sustaining of dependability and trustworthiness are far more likely motivated by expediency than by moral considerations. It is not so much adherence to moral principles which makes most men "live up to their commitments" as it is the dictate of prudence—fear of social censure, or of economic loss in the long run. The proverb, "Honesty is the best policy," underscores the fact that the most effective regulator in inter-collective relations is necessity rather than the morality preached from the pulpit.

Thus, it is of primary importance that we distinguish between commitment for the sake of expediency and commitment in its moral sense—commitment for its own sake, or in other words, commitment to commitment of self. By commitment to commitment of self, we mean that a person must live up to his commitments to others, not because of social necessity, but rather because of a prior commitment to self. By so doing, he demonstrates, at least to himself, that the intent of his agreement reflects his own free will and not a compliance with the conventions of social interrelations. Truthfulness, faithfulness, dependability are, then, seen as the result of a self-proposed purport rather than one which is imposed upon the parties to the agreement by the requirements inherent in the conditions of the agreement. For agreements between individuals to be designated as commitments in the moral sense, they must be grounded in a prior commitment to self. This gives us a general maxim by which the ethical agent must be guided in his relations with others: *Relate yourself to others in such a fashion that the purport of your intent flows from a commitment to commitment.* This maxim applies with equal force to the ethical agent's relations to himself. Here it takes on the form: *Act in such a fashion that the determination of your action flows from a commitment to commitment.* We call this the principle of self-determination.

Since commitment to the truth of self is the decisive factor which determines *moral* conduct, it constitutes the ground in which all other virtues are rooted. This implies the demand that the virtues we are

93

called upon to practice in relation to others must first be made applicable to one's relations to self.

Take the virtue of love, for example. A person cannot be said to love his neighbor if he is unable to love himself. Commentators have pointed out that the Biblical command, "Love thy neighbor *as thyself*," implies the requirement of self-love. Self-love is the prerequisite condition for the love of others. Erich Fromm has given us an incisive analysis of different types of love, distinguishing essentially between symbiotic forms, which are either masochistic or sadistic in nature, and the "productive" one, which springs from a proper love of self.* What holds true of love holds equally true of related attributes, such as compassion, kindness, sympathy, empathy, etc.

Or take, for example, the virtue of justice. A person cannot be said to do justice to the needs of others if he is unable to do justice to his own essential needs and basic interests. In the context of self-actualization, justice implies the demand to give full rein to the expression of one's potentialities. Justice in the sense of rectitude or just dealings of men with each other applies with equal force to one's dealings in relation to self. To do right by oneself is primary to doing right to others.

Or finally, take the virtue of charity, which is customarily taken to be benevolence or good will to the poor and suffering, or leniency in judging the actions or attitudes of others. Again, in the context of self-actualization, charity can be seen as the moral imperative to be lenient or tolerant in respect to one's limitations and the inevitable failures and frustrations which one encounters in the explorative enterprise of realizing the vision of one's self-proposed life-form of being.

Our explication of commitment in the context of character can be seen to shed light especially on the controversy between theorists who are loosely called descriptivists and those who are grouped as prescriptivists. The controversy is centered in the issue whether or not moral judgments, like all other judgments, are descriptive in character, or, in other words, whether or not the key moral terms contained in a given value judgment are analyzable by reference to

---

* Erich Fromm, *Man for Himself*, Holt, Rinehart and Winston, New York, Seventeenth Printing, April 1964, pp. 107-112.

94

relevant empirical matters of fact. Broadly speaking, descriptivists hold, as C. D. Broad puts it, that "moral characteristics are always dependent on other characteristics which can be described in purely neutral non-moral terms."* The descriptivists are generally inclined to view or to make of ethics a science like the rest of the sciences, distinctive only in respect to its subject matter, which would tend to make it a branch of psychology in particular or the social sciences in general.

The prescriptivists, on the other hand, insist that while moral terms may have a certain descriptive meaning, their essential characteristic lies in their prescriptive, rather than descriptive import. Moral judgments are prescriptive because they do not so much describe attitudes and behavior patterns as they prescribe what men ought to do under given circumstances. Moral judgments are not designed to be *descriptions* of behavior patterns and principles which govern most men in their conduct, but rather *prescriptions* or moral guides of conduct for the kind of person who intends to act in a moral way. They are of the nature of moral imperatives calling for certain kinds of action in the resolution of moral conflicts.

Clearly, the recognition of commitment as the decisive factor in determining moral conduct makes descriptivism an untenable position. With commitment seen as an overriding determination to create a unique individuality, thereby making moral values unique to the individual, their reduction to purely empirical data becomes fallacious.

We have seen that, given certain conditions, moral judgments must be taken to be action guiding in character enabling the ethical agent to choose an appropriate course of action. In this respect we agree with the prescriptivists. However, we depart from them in insisting that what makes moral judgments prescriptive is not so much the fact that they are action-guiding, but that they are grounded in a prior commitment by the ethical agent to act on them, or, in other words, to abide by the dictate of his own moral reasoning. Moral judgments, then, can be said to be prescriptive only if they flow from a dynamic character structure which, as it were, commits its

---

* See his article, "Some of the Main Problems of Ethics," In *Readings in Philosophical Analysis,* Appleton-Century-Crofts, Inc., New York, 1949, p. 551.

possessor to make his moral valuation conform to his moral conduct.

The failure to recognize that moral judgments must be grounded in commitment to be described as "action-guiding" accounts for certain fallacies detectable in the writings of some of the leading prescriptivists today. Take, for example, the following statement by C. L. Stevenson, in which he seems to side with the prescriptivists: "The many theorists who have refused to identify ethical statements with scientific ones have much to be said in their favor. They have seen that ethical judgments mold or alter attitudes, rather than describe them. . . ."* Our analysis of moral judgments in the context of moral character has made it quite clear that it is fallacious to assume that "moral judgments mold or alter attitudes." So far from molding or altering attitudes, moral judgments are utterly impotent so long as they lack the support of a prior commitment which can flow only from dynamic character.

Or take, for example, the characterization of prescriptivity by one of its leading proponents, R. M. Hare. It reflects the same fallacy which we detected in Stevenson's statement. Hare describes "the ethical theory" which he sets forth in his book, *Freedom and Reason,* as "a type of prescriptivism, in that it maintains that it is one of the characteristics of moral terms, and one which is a sufficiently essential characteristic for us to call it part of the meaning of these terms, that judgments containing them are, as typically used, intended as *guides to conduct.*"** Here again, we note the prescriptivist's thesis that moral judgments *per se* can be taken to be guides to moral conduct. Underlying this assumption is the naive belief that the instruction we derive from moral judgments made by one whom we respect can have a determinate influence on us. This is clear from the following paragraph:

> Now what happens if we try to add prescriptive meaning to such a word? The inevitable consequence of such an addition is that the descriptive meaning-rule becomes more than a mere meaning-rule. . . The rule will still say that it is proper to apply

---

* Charles L. Stevenson, "The Nature of Ethical Disagreement," op. cit. p. 593.

** R. M. Hare, *Freedom and Reason,* Oxford University Press, 1963, p. 67 (Italics are my own.)

the word 'good' to a certain kind of man; but in saying this (in enunciating the rule) we shall be doing more than specify-ing the meaning of the word. For in saying that it is proper to call a certain kind of man good (for example a man who feeds his children, does not beat his wife, etc.) we are not just ex-plaining the meaning of a word; it is not mere verbal instruc-tion that we are giving, but something more: *moral* instruction. In learning that, of all kinds of man, *this* one can be called good, our hearer will be learning something synthetic, a moral principle. It will be synthetic because of the added prescriptive-ness of the word 'good'; in learning it, he will be learning, not merely to use a word in a certain way, but to commend, or prescribe for imitation, a certain kind of man. A man who wholeheartedly accepts such a rule is likely to *live,* not merely *talk,* differently from one who does not. Our descriptive mean-ing-rule has thus turned into a synthetic moral principle.*

Hare fails to realize that "moral instruction" is utterly unreliable as a guide to moral action. As Aristotle has taught us, the prescrip-tivity of moral judgments resides in the character of the man, in a moral determination cultivated by persistent moral action, and not, as Hare naively assumes, "in learning" about certain moral rules or the usage of certain moral terms. While Hare persistently refers to commitment in his analysis of prescriptivity, he takes it for granted, as if the meaning were self-explanatory. He assumes that a man who commits himself to the acceptance of a certain moral principle neces-sarily applies it in the determination of his conduct. He fails to realize that unless commitment is grounded in dynamic character (Hare's book makes no reference to character structure), it cannot be said to have moral quality. The failure to first explicate the nature of moral commitment, before applying it to the resolution of moral problems, is a typical instance of the fallacy of misplaced primacy. Hare's entire thesis of the "logical universalizability" of moral judg-ment is predicated upon the assumption of commitment. It is based on an analogy, in which what holds true for empirical statements is said to hold true, to a certain extent, for moral statements. Just as in

---

* *Ibid,* p. 23.

descriptive statements a man who says that "X is red" is committed to the proposition "everything like this in the relevant respect is red," so too, in moral judgments a man is expected "to ask of his own actions, 'To what action can I commit myself in this situation, realizing that, in committing myself to it, I am also (because the judgment is a universalizable one) prescribing to anyone in a like situation to do the same—in short, what can I will to be a universal law?' "*

The surreptitious injection of the term of commitment, drawn from an analogy with empirical statements, into moral judgments places Hare's position on precarious grounds.

Broadly speaking, Hare's thesis is that the combination of the logical principle of universalizability and the moral principle of prescriptivity commit a man to the proposition: ". . . But if I think that I ought to do A in these circumstances, I am committed to thinking that anyone else similarly placed ought to do the same."** "I have argued," he says, "that moral judgments, when intended seriously and with full force, must be taken as committing the speaker to some universal judgment applying to anyone in a relevantly similar situation."***

It is evident that Hare's position reflects the futile effort of establishing universality in ethics. The applicability of his purely logical principle of universalizability is, at best, a trivial one, considering the complexities of the human situation and the uniqueness of individual character. No two moral situations are alike, not even in the more essential aspects of the circumstances. The triviality of Hare's principle of universalizability is in large part the result of the attempt to make moral judgments analogous to empirical statements. It is basically attributable to his failure to carefully explicate the moral nature of commitment in the context of moral character. The force of moral commitment is in no way a logical one, but rather one grounded in a deliberately cultivated dynamic personality structure. We have seen that its import involves primarily the resolution of moral conflicts which are relevant to the ethical agent alone. The untenability of Hare's position lies in his naive assumption that uni-

---

* *Ibid*, pp. 47-48.
** *Ibid*, p. 71.
*** *Ibid*.

versalizability and prescriptivity jointly prove "sufficient for establishing the rationality of morals. . . ."* We reiterate in this context
that rationality in ethics is grounded not in abstract principles but
rather in the limited base of a dynamic character structure. This
naiveté is equally evident in his assertion that, "ethics (i.e. the logic
of moral language) is an immensely powerful engine for producing
moral agreement; for if two people are willing to use the moral
word 'ought,' and to use it in the same way (viz. the way that I
have been describing), the other possible sources of moral disagreement are all eliminable."**

Hare's qualification, "if two people are willing to use the moral
word 'ought,' and to use it in the same way (viz. the way that I have
been describing), the other possible sources of moral disagreement
are all eliminable,"*** is a tall order, which cannot simply be filled
by wishful thinking. Not only does Hare seem oblivious of C. Stevenson's significant distinction between disagreement in belief and disagreement in attitude,**** but he lacks the significant distinction
between moral reasoning as it applies to moral conflicts in relation
to oneself and moral conflicts in relation to others. Nor does he
distinguish between the logical apparatus of moral reasoning in the
resolution of moral conflicts which involve the ethical agent only
and moral conflicts which arise from conflicting claims of opposing
parties.

To what absurdities Hare's position can lead an ethical thinker
is evident in his attempt to analyze the possible bearing of his principles of prescriptivity and universalizability on a hypothetical argu-
ment between a liberal and a Nazi engaged in the policy of the
extermination of the Jew.†

"The real difficulty," Hare asserts, "of making a moral decision
is, as I have said before, that of finding some action to which one
is prepared to commit oneself, and which at the same time one is
prepared to accept as exemplifying a principle of action binding on

---

* *Ibid,* p. 18.
** *Ibid,* p. 97.
*** *Ibid.*
**** See footnote in Chap. 5, p. 6, above.
† See his chapter, Chap. 9 Part 2, on Toleration and Fanaticism, esp.
pp. 158-178.

anyone in like circumstances. This is what makes the moral life, for one who takes it seriously, so appallingly difficult."*

This is not at all the difficulty of the moral life as we see it. Rather than the search for possible universal principles to which one can make one's actions conform, the real difficulty of the moral life lies in the search for a truth of being which constitutes the vision of one's life-form, and to the realization of which a man must devote the whole of himself. The real difficulty of the moral life lies in the construction of dynamic character along the lines of differentiation and integration. In this deliberate constructive endeavor alone, moral reasoning can be made constructively and dynamically operative. In moral conflicts between opposing parties, moral reasoning is impotent so long as it is not reinforced by certain dynamic character aspects in the individuals involved in the conflict. It is evident that while contemporary moral thinkers are cognizant of this fact, they lose sight of it in their absorption in the subtle analyses of the meaning of moral terms.

Hare's basic weakness is characteristic of a dominant group of ethical thinkers today (of which he is an eminent representative), those who believe that ethics' basic objective is the logical analysis of moral language. Unless we cease to divorce moral discourse from moral character and begin to reconstruct, in the light of current insights into the science of man, the abiding theses of the classical tradition, especially its emphasis on the interconnection of personality structure and moral values, there is little hope for pioneering advances in ethical inquiry. In the light of our discussion, the futility of an explication of moral values or moral judgments outside of the context of the ethical agent seems fairly obvious. For all intents and purposes, the import of moral judgments appears to be void of meaningfulness, in an ethical sense, if they are analyzed in isolation, separate and apart from the ethical agent whose valuation they represent.

It is difficult to see what possible insight can be gained for the elucidation of basic issues in ethics from a logical analysis of moral terms or judgments totally unrelated to essential aspects of the ethical situation as a whole. We have seen that if moral values or moral

---

* *Ibid,* p. 73.

judgments are to be meaningful as guides to moral conduct, they must derive from a prior commitment which alone is action-determining in character. Furthermore, moral judgments are relevant guides of moral conduct only for the ethical agent who makes these judgments in the resolution of moral conflicts involving problems that concern him alone. It is true that they may indirectly have a bearing on others, but whatever this bearing may be, it is of no significance to the ethical agent's valuation or the determination of his action. All this, of course, is the basic implication of a theory, which, while it denies the objectivity or cognitive import of moral values or judgments, *per se,* does not rule out rationality in ethics altogether, but seeks to establish it within the framework of an objective relativism.

CHAPTER SEVEN

The Ethical Man

LORD, who shall abide in Thy tabernacle? who shall dwell in Thy holy hill?

He that walketh uprightly, and worketh righteousness, and speaketh the truth in his heart.

He that backbiteth not with his tongue, nor doeth evil to his neighbor, nor taketh up a reproach against his neighbor.

In whose eyes a vile person is contemned; but he honoreth them that fear the LORD. He that sweareth to his own hurt, and changeth not.

He that putteth not out his money to usury, nor taketh reward against the innocent. He that doeth these things shall never be moved.

PSALMS 15

THE STATURE of the ethical man has come into full view. It is seen as an emergent form in a creative evolution of selfhood, in which the will to be free is the prime moving force. It is an ever-evolving structure, in which the traditional virtues, functioning as the instrumentalities of character construction, are so utilized as to give rise to uniqueness, individuality, novelty, and creativity. Reflecting an inner harmony and singularity of purpose, this stature of the ethical man establishes the dignity of the individual and the worth of human existence. The ethical man, as an emergent form of self-realization, is both an idealization of man in every age and a challenge to man, especially in our age, in which a creeping impersonalization, as Kierkegaard forewarned us, has made anonymity the saving virtue, collectivity the saving refuge, and mass opinion the criterion of truth.

The ethical man is first and foremost the *free* man, free not because of a political endowment with the inalienable right to liberty, but rather because of the establishment of independence and self-mastery in the practical sphere of life.

The ethical man is the *self-reliant man,* drawing on his own resources—his potentialities and talents—for the satisfaction of his needs and interests.

The ethical man is the man of *truth,* a unique truth which he has not only fashioned by himself, but in the quest of which he is seen to implement those virtues which infuse human existence with purpose and ultimate meaning.

The ethical man is the man of *commitment;* he has entered into a covenant with himself, a covenant so binding that from it he can draw the power, the moral determination to actualize his self-proposed truth, his self-created essence of being.

The ethical man is the man of *courage,* the courage to be himself, the courage to stand alone, if need be, in a battle of resistance against dominant pressures.

The ethical man is the *productive* man, not only by creating an individuality unique to himself, but by making it a reservoir of productivity for progress and human welfare.

The ethical man is the *marginal* man who, unbound by tradition or custom, not only reflects critically on his culture's dominant values, but recasts them to adapt them to his own purposes and goals.

The posture of the ethical man in his society is firm and unequivocal. He is not swayed by heroic enthusiasms, nor is he paralyzed by timid doubts or uncertainty. Not blinded by prejudice or emotional bias, he examines all issues carefully. He neither rushes into a decision nor backs away from one. Engrossed in his own creative pursuits, he neither meddles in the affairs of others nor brooks interference with his own. A whole man, at peace with himself, he fights no wars of aggression with others. The critic of his own achievements, he is immune to the plaudits of the crowd, and craves not the approval of his peers. The judge of his own actions, he is uninfluenced by the opinions of others, nor does he sit in judgment over the conduct of his fellow men. A man with a mission, he is not a missionary. A man with a cause, he is not a crusader. A man with a vision, he is not a prophet.

Standing, more often than not, alone, the ethical man is not the lonely stranger in a crowd. In his aloneness there is nothing of the terrible sense of loneliness of the fragmented man today. His is of an entirely different quality. His is a solitude of communion with self, reflective of the man who "dwells on the holy hill," who, removed from the prosaic preoccupations of his contemporaries, quietly and boldly pursues his chosen course of destiny. All too frequently, the ethical man stands alone because his commitment to self compels him to take a position from which the majority will cowardly back away. At times suffused with agony, his aloneness girds him with a towering strength which cannot so easily be moved from its foundations. Though smaller men seem irresistibly compelled to test the fibre of such strength, the ethical man can endure the trial of assault because his stature is rooted in an indomitable faith in himself and in his cause. An alien, perhaps, in his social environs, he is at home in a wider realm of his own fashioning whence none can dislodge him.

Transcending the parochial boundaries of his generation, the ethical man is its conscience, the solitary voice in a mass chorus of conformity. He is, as it were, civilization itself, shattering traditions and rebuilding them on new foundations. He is the Socratic gadfly, whose probing mind may provoke the more serious around him to inquiry and critical reexamination of their own pet notions and favorite presuppositions.

In human intercourse the ethical man is so constituted as to be free from symbiotic relationships in which individuals are seen to exploit each other's needs. His interdependence with others is based not on need, but on genuine fellowship and growth. Unlike most men, he is not prone to transfer to his fellow men his own frustrations. His discontent, so far from embittering him, stirs him to greater effort. Doing justice to his own needs, he is sensitized to the needs of others. A proper love of self renders him susceptive to brotherly love. Accepting himself, with all his peculiarities, he is tolerant of the foibles in others.

He quests no power over those who come within his sphere of influence, but rather inspires them with his own confidence and inner strength. He is compassionate toward his neighbors' weaknesses and appreciative of their strengths. He is keenly aware that to judge another, one would need to emphatically enter into his very being, take the other's place, and view his actions in the total context of circumstance, intent, and perspective. So he suspends judgment, and rather than being critical of the deeds of others, focuses his criticism on a persistent appraisal of his own actions.

Committed to a truth which is grounded in his being, the ethical man is the true man in every sense of the word. He is the true man in the sense of being veracious, in contrast to one who is dishonest. "He speaketh the truth in his heart." He scrupulously adheres to the strictures of theoretical truth in speech as well as in practice. His statements have factual correctness. He makes no assertions so long as he is not in full possession of the facts. In his actions he is committed to the elimination of all possible deceptions, even those arising from inadvertent error or oversight.

The ethical man is the true man in the sense of being just, in contrast to one who is unfair. "He sweareth to his own hurt and changeth not." Not only can he be safely trusted to live up to his commitments, but his sense of justice prevails over considerations of self-interest. Neither a utilitarian nor an altruist, he does justice to both ethical attitudes. He pursues his own interest so long as it is not detrimental to the well-being of others, but he is capable of surrendering his self-interest when it is injurious to others.

The ethical man is the true man in the sense of being upright, in contrast to one who is unscrupulous. "He that walketh uprightly." His appearance is at one with his reality. His actions conform to his principles and norms.

The ethical man is the true man in the sense of being righteous, in contrast to one who is base or wicked. "He worketh righteousness." He is committed to a sense of righteousness which makes him an active proponent of the rights of others. Not only does he respect the rights of others, but he will not stand idly by when his fellow man is treated wrongfully. He will speak up in defense of the wronged individual and take action if it is in his power to do so.

The ethical man is the man who sees humanity in every human being. To him an individual is a person with distinctive needs and aspirations, and never just a representative of a collective aggregate of people.

In his total relations with others, the ethical man translates into practice the Kantian maxim: "*Act so that in your own person, as*

105

*well as in the person of any other, you are treating mankind also as an end, never merely as a means."**

The possessor of the autonomous traits of self-confidence, self-respect, and self-knowledge, the ethical man needs no "mask" behind which to hide his identity. Unlike most of his contemporaries, who are cloaked in the protective garb of title or office or the role assigned to them by their society, deriving from an "artificial personality" a feigned dignity or pomp, the ethical man seeks identification only with his own individuality. His is the genuine dignity of man, which requires no special status symbols for its support. Thus, the ethical man is the man who communicates from the center of his personality, from the essence of his being. While he claims the right to discriminate in choosing his companions, the ethical man creates, once he enters into fellowship, genuine interpersonal relations. The Epicurean ideal of friendship is one of his prized values; his social companions can safely rely on him for the loyalty and trust of a true friend. Though capable of compassion, he does not indulge his comrade's tendency to self-pity, but rather helps rebuild, whenever possible, a shaken faith in self. Nor does he flatter an inflated ego, but rather provokes sober self-scrutiny. From the shared experience of creative growth in authentic fellowship, the ethical man derives a large measure of the joy of living.

The stature of the ethical man has cosmic dimensions. His transcendence of tradition and convention makes him keenly cognizant of his universal role, of man's place in the cosmos, of man's distinct interrelation with the total universe. Neither a mere devotee of a particular theology nor the typical atheist, whose break with a theological tradition reflects psychological rebellion rather than a constructive quest of selfhood, the ethical man quests a God faith of his own creation. Reaching for self-fulfillment, he fully understands that he must invest the universe with an ontological perfectibility. His conception of self as a creative evolution of selfhood is incommensurate with a cosmic view which conceives of being as a flux of random events devoid of purpose and meaningful direction. He is aware of chaotic existential phenomena, as well as manifest underlying uni-

---

* Immanuel Kant, *The Fundamental Principles of the Metaphysic of Ethics.*

formities and regularities of law. Himself a creative process in the making, he finds his universe a dynamic process in which the emergence of creativity and novelty is the essential aspect of being. Impatient with incompleteness and seeking to approximate perfection, he endows the cosmos with ultimate meaning. These perspectives become, as it were, the ingredients of a reconstructed God faith. While it is possible for the ethical man to adhere to the tenets of agnosticism, since his self-reliance makes him look to himself, not only for creative growth, but also for the coping with the contingent adversities of existence, he is not likely to abide with a God idea whose existence or essence is unknown or unknowable. Since he is committed to the reconstruction of traditional ideas by infusing them with fresh meanings, he is more likely to invest his traditional God concept, the one he inherited from his theological background, with a meaningfulness commensurate with his self-designed total outlook on life. His peculiar aloneness within his society, his marginality, will make him quest for an at-homeness in the universe, an immovable anchorage in the cosmos. In his creative evolution to selfhood, he will shatter many God ideas before he enters into an abiding communion with his God.

The ethical man may evolve to a metaphysical God idea akin to Whitehead's conception of the deity as "both the primordial and consequent nature"* of a creative, organic process, where God is seen "to share with every new creation its actual world"** and where creatureliness "is objectified in God as a novel element in God's objectification of that actual world."*** God may be to him the eternal ground of his being in the ultimate advance of human creative possibilities. Or he may fashion for himself a more personalized God idea, in which God is seen as the universal personality with whom the human personality can enter into an "I-Thou" communion of intimate and direct fellowship. Or he may find his faith in a humanistic God idea akin to Dewey's, where God is seen as the ultimate unity of man's noblest ideals and aspirations. But whatever his ultimate God idea, it will be reflective of the ethical man's unique creative perspective of life and the universe as a whole.

---

* A. N. Whitehead, *Process and Reality*, Harper and Row, New York, 1960, p. 523.
** *Ibid.*
*** *Ibid.*

As the solitary bastion of personal freedom in today's dominant society, the ethical man is the single hope of human freedom tomorrow. With automation replacing the usefulness of human productivity, the creative endeavors of the ethical man in constructing dynamic individuality establish, in this technological age, new dimensions of human creativity. The prophetic vision of the ethical man as the foundation of his generation and the hope for human survival has never been so pertinent and crucial to human destiny as it is in this day of mechanization and impersonalization of human existence.

Index